Reflective Music Teaching

Ideas for Early-Career Music Teachers

Erik Piazza
John Mills
Danny Ziemann

©2020 Low Down Publishing

All Rights Reserved.

No part of this publication may be reproduced, stored in retrieval system, or transmitted, in any form or by any means, electronic, mechanical, photocopying, recording or otherwise, without prior written permission from Low Down Publishing.

Trademark notice: Product or corporate names may be trademarks or registered trademarks, and are used only for identification and explanation without intent to infringe.

ISBN: 978-1-7353277-0-9

Editing: Erik Piazza & John Mills
Cover Design: Alison Coté
Interior Layout: Lauren Woodrow
Foreword: Ann Marie Stanley, Ph.D.

For supplemental materials and information, please visit:
www.LowDownPublishing.com

Please consider reviewing this book on Amazon. Our goal is to connect with as many educators as possible, and we welcome your feedback. Thank you!

Acknowledgements

This book would not have been possible without the support of the Institute for Music Leadership at the Eastman School of Music. We thank them for their generous financial backing and advice throughout the publishing process.

We would also like to thank our amazing music teachers and mentors for influencing our perspectives. They went above and beyond to create an atmosphere of joyous music making and learning, embodying the ethos of lifelong learners. To them, we are forever grateful.

We wrote this book to help guide you through the many joys and challenges in teaching. You are a critical part of the music education community, and we hope you find this resource helpful.

Table of Contents

Foreword vii

Introduction—*Begin by Reflecting* xi

Chapter 1—*Getting Started* 1
   General Ideas 1
   Music-Specific Ideas 5
   Scenarios 8
   Summary 17

Chapter 2—*Unpacking Assumptions* 18
   Common Misconceptions 19
   Scenarios 22
   Summary 34

Chapter 3—*Critical Self-Reflection* 35
   Scenario 35
   Reflecting on Successes and Challenges 37
   Innovate with Student Learning in Mind 39
   Staying Informed 42
   Coda 49

Chapter 4—*Relating Curriculum to Community* 50
- Facilitating Relatable Activities 51
- Scenarios 52
- Summary 60

Chapter 5—*Creative Musical Activities* 62
- Understanding the Creative Process 64
- Defining Creativity 65
- Generative Musical Activities 66
- Ideas about Music Technology 67
- Scenario 69
- Music Technology ↔ Creative Musical Activities 73
- Staying Open to Different Musics 74
- Making Music to Share Music 76
- Resources 77

Chapter 6—*Synthesizing Ideas* 79
- Three Example Projects 80
- Feedback 84

Notes 87
References 92

Foreword

So you want to be a music teacher. Congratulations! You've chosen one of the most creative, collaborative, and rewarding professions out there. But learning to be a great music educator is an undeniably challenging endeavor, requiring immense skill and good judgment. You'll have to find and draw upon your personal reserve of strength, musicianship, and what my grandma would call *gumption*: clever, spirited resourcefulness. There will be times in your teacher preparation program—and the first few years of teaching—when you will need a mentor, a counselor, a role model, and a nap (and at some point you should get all of those things!). There will also be times in your teacher preparation program—and the first few years of teaching—when you will need the helpful information in this book.

I'm happy Erik, John, and Danny wrote it for you.

I'm glad you were smart enough to pick it up for your learning today, and for your future reference.

And just for some variety in emotion: I'm sad that I have no crystal ball. But I do have a Magic 8 Ball™ and if I ask it: *"will readers benefit from this book?"* I get a strong *"all signs point to yes"* message. (In case you were wondering, the Magic 8 Ball™ had no comment on how many people would read this foreword.) Minus a real crystal ball, here are my predictions of how you will use this text now and in the future.

You'll read and re-read the various definitions and explanations of reflective teaching, until you come to your own convictions about how reflection is helpful to you in your own teaching practice. The authors have helpfully provided, at the end of each chapter, real-world scenarios with accompanying guided discussion. They prompt you to think about each story from your own emerging professional perspective. You'll begin to proudly own your identity as a reflective practitioner. You'll analyze and grow to understand, as the authors point out in Chapter 1, not just *how*, but *why* you make particular educational and musical choices.

But then, undoubtedly your thinking will be challenged by someone who has a different idea of what it means to reflect. An education professional (a professor, a principal, a co-worker) may ask you to engage in "reflective-ish" activities that are mandatory, can be assessed and evaluated according to some metric, and theoretically can be improved upon with enough hard work. I know as a professor I have assigned – and graded – the dreaded "one-page written reflection" over some reading or classroom observation. These type of reflections are not always personally meaningful or productive and they are boring as heck to read.

But the *self*-reflection espoused in this book is different: it can become a rock-solid basis for thoughtful teaching. When you forget the purpose or point of reflection, you can re-read Chapter 3 on "Critical Self-Reflection" to remind yourself of what *you* can accomplish by meaningfully reflecting. Find a sage collaborator (as Erik was for Addie, in Chapter 3), re-discover your journal, create an action research project, ask your students for feedback. You'll soon reconnect with your personal reflective practice.

At some point, you will need a reminder to reconsider and challenge long-held, almost subconscious assumptions about music teaching and learning. Refer to Chapter 2's list of misconceptions to see if you've fallen back into an unquestioning belief in tradition. There will be times when you can't relate to your students, and you seem to be rapidly losing their attentiveness. Check out Chapter 4 for reminders about how you can connect with people, form relationships, and design musical experiences that are relevant to your students' interests *and* coherent with your goals as an instructor. Chapter 5 will help you if you're stuck for ideas: it contains practical, contemporary perspectives on creativity, technology, and generative processes. If you really need a kick-in-the-pants, pick some of your most intelligent musician friends and recreate a discussion or debate around the themes from Scenario 5.1. You may be shocked, or inspired, by others' viewpoints; either way you'll be moved to action.

Whether you find yourself in need of a sample lesson for a job interview, a teaching demonstration, or a great long-term project for your students, the helpful synthesis and related projects in Chapter 6 are big-picture, creative, and technologically flexible. You can go back to this source for ideas, repeatedly. You may use the format as a template for your own creative and student-centered instructional design. Throughout the book, the authors' vivid and realistic depictions of teaching scenarios are a big bonus; strong norms of autonomy and privacy in music teaching have resulted in many music teachers never having had the benefit of an accurate and tangible window into the real-life questions that music teachers wrestle with daily. Reading the authors' rich accounts based on their own experience gives a strong sense of "being there." Reading those teaching dilemmas should bring you confidence and comfort as you embark on any new teaching assignment. You're not alone and you're probably *not* the first music teacher to have been faced with similar uncertainties.

The authors give you a lot of good material in Chapter 1 for how to get started, both for teaching in general and as a music teacher specifically. The length of this foreword should not be a thing standing between you and getting started on your terrific career as a music educator, so I will close with a great quote from Chapter 3: *You are capable of helping to advance the profession of music teaching and learning.*

And that's true: you are. Enjoy the book, and get started.

Ann Marie Stanley, Ph.D.
Associate Professor and Head of Music Education
Louisiana State University

Introduction

Begin by Reflecting

> *Why did you choose music?*
>
> *To teach? To learn? To make?*
>
> *What drives you? Who influences you?*
>
> *What is most important?*

Whether you joined our field through a love of music, a desire to help others, or by recognizing that music is a uniquely human experience, a career teaching music has the potential to be full of collaboration, creative expression, and joy.

We are excited to present *Reflective Music Teaching: Ideas for Early-Career Music Teachers,* a handbook of ideas for music teachers committed to considerate and inclusive practice. We present a variety of fictional scenarios, reflections, and ideas based on real-world experiences from our personal careers with the intent to help public, private, community, and collegiate music teachers. Our ideas are grounded in current research, and expressed in a simple narrative format.

We believe reflective practice in music education is essential. In this book, we encourage you to consider "the way it's always been done," and provide strategies for critical reflection. While established teaching practices may still hold value, the purpose of this book is to help you reconsider their merit. As you gain experience, the concepts in these six chapters will help you develop your own reflective teaching style.

We believe creative musical activities provide teachers with opportunities to practicalize the foundational ideas explored in the first four chapters. In Chapter 5, we turn to creative musical activities and the role of technology to support reflective and relevant music instruction.

Chapter 1: Getting Started
Explore general and music-specific ideas for early-career music teachers with an emphasis on practical tips for maintaining professional relationships with students and other stakeholders.

Chapter 2: Unpacking Assumptions
Consider the purposes and implications of common teaching practices. We discuss common misconceptions about prevalent music teaching practices, and pose questions to help you meet the individual needs of current students.

Chapter 3: Critical Self-Reflection
Celebrate your successes, reflect, and develop a plan moving forward. We offer important considerations as you become more comfortable in your position, ways you may continue to grow as a music teacher and learner, and how to use your influence to advance the profession.

Chapter 4: Relating Curriculum to Community
Design curriculum that directly connects to your students' backgrounds and goals. We encourage you to provide specific directions

and feedback, and prioritize students as you design curriculum. Base curricular decisions on meaningful traditions and positive relationships. Use your expertise to link your classes with the outside world.

Chapter 5: Creative Musical Activities
Facilitate activities centered around creativity and technology. Include improvising, composing, and arranging as regular components of your instruction. We discuss how learning communities and technologies interact to promote exploration and understanding of student-generated musical content.

Chapter 6: Synthesizing Ideas
Combine concepts from Chapters 1 through 5 when planning instruction. We offer three flexible project ideas as examples of creative musical activities that use various tools and technologies. We include templates for organizing feedback and sharing ideas.

Chapter 1

Getting Started

Whether you are preparing for a career teaching music or are brand new to the teaching field, you are likely to receive numerous unsolicited pearls of wisdom from more experienced music teachers and colleagues. We have personally heard (and have often perpetuated!) these timeless creeds, which are certainly worth incorporating in your teaching practice. In this chapter we offer practical ideas and recommendations to incorporate into your teaching practice, then conclude with scenarios for reflection. Although we generally direct the commentary toward music teachers in a primary or secondary school setting, these ideas also apply to community ensemble conductors, church music directors, and private lesson teachers.

General Ideas

Be yourself.
Remember that you are a qualified, educated, dedicated early-career music teacher, and there is no need to pretend to be someone you're not. Most students will see through a false persona and immediately recognize a lack of sincerity. Further, maintaining this façade on a daily basis can be exhausting! Learn to be comfortable teaching as yourself. You *can* be yourself while gaining the respect

of your students, and while running your classroom in a manner consistent with your beliefs and values.

Set expectations.
Establish your expectations from the start. Throughout the year, you will find it easier to scale back classroom expectations rather than to impose new ones mid-way through the year. Come up with non-negotiables for your classroom and encourage your students to share their own ideas and expectations. Also, you might use a less authoritarian term like "Classroom Norms" instead of "Rules" to promote student autonomy. Students are likely to adhere to norms—and more likely to understand consequences for breaking them—when they are co-constructed. Consider posting expectations near the front of the classroom to provide an easy way to manage behaviors. Reinforce through daily teaching. You will create a culture of respect when students know what they can expect from you, as well.

Learn your students' names quickly.
You may be familiar with the following quote: "Students don't care how much you know until they know how much you care." Give yourself one week to learn all of your students' names. It doesn't matter if you have 50 students or 300 students. You have one week. (Okay... you can take two weeks if you have more than 300 students, but you should check your contract. That's more than one teacher should have to manage, especially an early-career music teacher!) School secretaries, assistants, or counselors may be able to help you print a seating chart with pictures.

Learn your students' stories.
Once you learn each student's name, learn about their home life. Call home and share one positive story within the first month (or so!) of school. It is incredibly time-consuming to connect with every family, but it is the first step in engaging with the community in

which you work. Also, it is much easier to make a difficult phone call if you have already established a good relationship with a parent or guardian. As you learn more about students' home lives, you will better understand their actions and reactions. When you do have to correct or reprimand a student, understand that each child is the center of somebody else's whole world. Even when they misbehave, treat each student as you would like your own child to be treated. If you can figure out *why* a student acts a certain way, you will have an easier time managing that behavior. This starts by making personal and professional connections with students and their parents.

Borrow ideas from other teachers.

As an early-career music teacher, your feelings may range between completely prepared and completely overwhelmed. You may even feel both at the same time! Don't worry—these feelings are normal. Pay attention to what other teachers are doing in your building, and ask if you can observe their classes. While your personal philosophy may differ from these experienced teachers, they are bound to provide you with valuable information. Open communication with a veteran teacher can strengthen your sense of community with your colleagues. You may find other teachers are not accustomed to open lines of communication, but that should not deter you from reaching out to them.

Be a reflective practitioner.

Your experiences and personal opinions inform your teaching. It is important to realize that we often revert to teaching as we were taught. Music and pedagogy are continually passed down from teacher to student; the way you teach is influenced by your teacher's teacher. Reflecting on his early career as a band teacher, Randall Allsup wrote: "I taught the way I was taught and I certainly did not see my expertise as a problem."[1] Understand why you make particular choices about content, communication, style, etc.

Remember, you are preparing students for *their* future. Teaching practices popular when you were in school may be less relevant today. Video record yourself teaching at least once a month. As difficult (painful, even!) as it may be to watch, these recordings provide an opportunity to evaluate your teaching style and delivery. How do you transmit information, and how do your students come to understand content?

Part of being a reflective teacher includes soliciting and considering feedback from many people. Your supervisor may provide suggestions in the form of a formal observation or evaluation. You may ask a trusted colleague for their opinion on a new idea, or for advice with a challenging situation. Parents and students may offer their thoughts virtually or in person. Your ability to be objective and reflective as you continue to grow as a teacher will have a direct impact on how gracefully you are able to receive feedback.

Develop an organizational strategy.
Develop a systematic method for organizing your email, computer files, and physical files. Keep your personal files separate from your work files. If you are using a work-issued computer, that machine is likely intended to be used *only* for work related activity. It may be helpful to create folders in both your email client and your computer hard drive with labels such as "Administration," "Budget," "Grant Writing," "Lesson Plans," "Meeting Minutes," "Professional Development," and "Parent Information." Label your handouts with easy to identify names (e.g., "2019 Senior Choir Roster") to make it easy to search for files in subsequent years. It may also be helpful to print the file location in the footer of the handout to make it easier to find when you need to resend that file to a parent or colleague. You may find it beneficial to group these folders by year ("2020-21") or by category ("Instrument Forms" or "Inventory"). These can be duplicated every year.

Connect with support staff.

These amazing people keep organizations running! Administrative assistants know the inner workings of your program, and will be invaluable to you as you navigate your first teaching job. They can also help you book facilities, arrange transportation, order supplies, and can usually tell you whom to contact with specific questions. Be sure to show custodial and maintenance staff your appreciation as they empty garbage, sweep the floor, replace light bulbs, deliver packages, cut the grass, or fix broken doors. Counselors help students navigate the difficulties of growing up — including problems at home, mental health issues, self-destructive thoughts, or coping with loss — all the issues you may not be trained or qualified to mediate.

Make connections with these essential staff members, and focus on the job you were hired to do. For a community of learners to function highly, everyone participating needs to be treated with respect and honor.[2] The quality of the adult relationships — which set the standard for expectations of student relationships — are essential to build a community of learners.

Music-Specific Ideas

So far, the advice in this chapter has been directed toward the teaching profession in general. As music teachers, we must consider practice-specific ideas that are relevant to students' musical growth. The following ideas may help you recognize your own bias and assumptions (discussed further in Chapter 2) inherent in many teaching practices.

Uncover your students' musical interests and goals.

This concept builds on learning your students' stories. Ask your students why they chose to take your class and what they hope to learn before assuming you know what is best for them. Structure your class to help them expand their musical interests and set their own musical goals, and incorporate these into your curriculum. Not all students will be immediately able to form concrete goals, but they will learn to develop them as you facilitate myriad musical experiences. Your priority should be to support and enrich your students' musical journeys. Use your expertise to help them discover their musical interests and goals.

Share your passions.

Students love to be around teachers with positive attitudes, and are inspired by those who teach with passion. If you are naturally drawn to a particular type of music or style — even if it's not necessarily part of your class — share it with your students! Your students are likely to feed off your passion for avant-garde jazz or mbira music even if they have not yet learned to appreciate it. Create opportunities for your students to love what you love. Encourage your students to do the same for you.

Be mindful when defining "quality" music.

The focus of many performance curricula is to teach students to perform classics like Bach and Mozart, Sousa and Grainger, or Ellington and Basie. When choosing repertoire, you are also choosing to exclude other musical works. It is important to consider how well your choices reflect students' lived experiences. Solicit their input when choosing music for your performance ensembles. Invite them to share some of their favorite music in class. Take this one step further and teach students to arrange their favorite music for your ensemble (see Chapter 5 for more on creativity). There are many approaches to choosing which music to learn about, remix, or perform, and including their musical interests will help promote learner autonomy.

Identify curricular stakeholders.

These are the people who will have input on your curriculum. F. Michael Connelly and D. Jean Clandinin assert "our job as teachers is to know who the stakeholders are and what stakes they have in our programs so we can be appropriately responsive."[3] The most obvious stakeholders may be your administrators: the principal, the fine arts director, or an administrator assigned to supervise music. Become familiar with their policies and expectations, as their opinions are more important to your career than those of your colleagues or predecessors.

It is also important to consider other stakeholders when designing and developing the scope and sequence of your curriculum. To whom are you accountable? Whose opinions should you consider when making curricular decisions? In addition to administration, consider the roles your students, their parents, your colleagues, the school board, community members, the government, taxpayers, colleges and universities, and local businesses may serve in determining course content.

Maintain detailed records.
Keep track of test scores, enrollment numbers, and lesson plans, and use them to inform your own practice. There is a difference between measuring a student's progress on a given activity and evaluating a student's success — not everything requires a grade, but you should have justification for every grade.[4] Use this data to track student progress and refine lesson plans. Ask students to self-reflect on performances, class activities, and assessments. Their perceptions of growth are difficult to quantify, but you may discover something more important than any number of scales or musical vocabulary: a growing love of music and appreciation of your program! These records will also help you advocate for your program.

Be a music maker.
You are what you repeatedly do. To maintain your musical skill set, stay involved in musical activities outside of your job. With a little searching, you may find established music groups in your area, such as community bands, orchestras, and choirs. You could also

set up a music studio at home. Anything that helps you maintain and develop new skills will allow you to keep growing. Alternatively, consider forming your own ensemble of any type. Your students will appreciate and respect your continued involvement in the world of making music, and you can invite them to your performances.

Scenarios

In this section, we present two hypothetical scenarios. We encourage you to consider how you might react if confronted with similar situations. For each story, think about the implications and consequences of the fictional music teachers' actions. Following each story, we review and discuss the choices made by the music teachers. Imagine how different choices might lead to a more desirable outcome.

The first scenario is about Alex, a third-year college student who teaches guitar lessons at the local music store. In the second scenario, Conny is a first-year teacher at a small public school who experiences her first annual evaluation with the building principal.

Scenario 1.1: Music Store Lessons

Alex is a jazz guitarist who just finished his third year of undergraduate study. He recently moved into his first off-campus apartment, and got a job teaching summer music lessons at a local music store. Eli is one of Alex's young guitar students, an enthusiastic 13-year old taking lessons for the first time. Eli's parents dropped him off at his first lesson with his brand new guitar, a digital tuner, and a Beatles Greatest Hits tablature book. The first few lessons went rather well. Alex taught Eli the basics of packing and unpacking, string names, how to tune the guitar, and a couple of basic chords — the same things Alex learned when he was just getting started. Alex explained how important it was to establish a consistent practice routine, and showed Eli how to track his progress using a weekly practice log. Eli was really eager to learn, and tried hard to complete the weekly melodic etude and chordal assignments.

However, Eli's enthusiasm began to deteriorate after a few months. Eli continued to bring his tablature book to lessons, even though Alex believed standard notation was far more beneficial to the development of music literacy. Eli continued to have difficulty tuning by himself, and he still couldn't transition between G, C, and D major chords without pausing. Each week, Alex felt like he had to reteach the same material over and over, and it appeared that Eli's progress had completely stalled. Alex found himself losing interest in his student, as his student lost interest in guitar.

Reflection

In hindsight, it may be easy to recognize some of the prior experiences and assumptions driving Alex's actions. However, it is often much harder to navigate such situations in the moment, and it is difficult to anticipate the effect of any given action.

Prior learning experiences often shape current teaching practices. Pierre Bourdieu's concept of *habitus* illuminates this process. Habitus refers to the process of internalizing and representing our social understanding of the world. Jeffrey Sallaz describes habitus as *prereflexive*.[5] In other words, the choices we make are often not the products of conscious thought, but rather emerge from a sense of learned responsiveness. Alex replicated elements of his childhood experiences, which he may have considered important to his development into a professional guitar teacher. It is easy to understand how Alex might have felt it was his responsibility to provide Eli with similar experiences so that he might experience the same level of success.

If we were able to offer feedback to Alex, we would encourage him to consider the music-specific advice offered in the beginning of this chapter.

What were Eli's musical interests and goals?

For Eli, whose attitude toward learning guitar was less serious than Alex expected, a more exploratory approach with varied learning experiences may have been more meaningful than the teacher-directed assignments. Students may not value daily practice until they start to recognize their progress. Had Alex considered a more aesthetic approach — centered around music appreciation and exploratory learning — Eli might have learned to appreciate the importance of diligent practicing. Alex could have fostered a greater appreciation for music by shepherding Eli towards new recordings, books, or even local concerts. Music teachers are responsible for guiding students along their musical journey.

Alex also assumed that Eli shared similar goals for learning guitar, but failed to consider Eli's reasons for studying guitar. Not every student aspires to be a professional musician, and student success may be measured by many different benchmarks. In this scenario, Alex failed to consider Eli's motives for learning guitar. This conflict between expectations and motivations may have led to feelings of resentment for both teacher and student.

Be mindful when defining "quality" music.

Eli brought a Beatles Greatest Hits tablature book, yet Alex ignored this and instead assigned weekly melodic and chordal exercises. It is possible to teach most musical elements (rhythmic reading, notation, form, dynamics, articulation, style, etc.) through any type of music. Instead of teaching Eli scales in isolation, Alex might have taught him to play one of the melodies from the tablature book. In fact, Alex missed many opportunities to help Eli develop his musical voice — we will discuss the importance of providing creative musical experiences for students in more depth in Chapter 5.

Who are the curricular stakeholders in this situation?
As we stated earlier in the chapter, it is not always simple to identify specific people with a legitimate stake in music instruction. Stakeholders closest to "Student" are most important, and decrease in importance as they move outwards. Yet, each concentric circle serves to support the student.

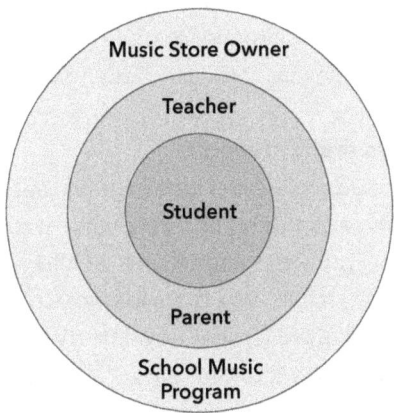

In this scenario, Alex might have consulted and involved Eli's parents. The parents not only pay for Eli's lessons, but they likely had some role in purchasing the instrument and books. It would have been helpful to discover what expectations they had for Eli's music lessons. Alex might have found the time to ask Eli's parents any of the following questions:

- "Has Eli shared any of what he does in lessons with you?"
- "How often do you see Eli practicing?"
- "Does Eli seem enthusiastic about learning music?"
- "Is there anything else that would be helpful for me to know about Eli's musical goals?"

Alex did not actively encourage parent participation—the backbone of some pedagogical approaches (e.g., the Suzuki method). Parents who are involved in their child's learning are able to celebrate success and encourage students throughout the week. Involving other stakeholders and support systems (e.g., the music store owner, the school music program) may have helped Eli continue to feel motivated and successful.

It is important for teachers to identify and include student goals into instruction, and keep students involved in the process. When students understand the rationale for pedagogical decisions, they are more likely to persevere through challenging activities.[6]

Had Eli's progress really stalled?

Not only do many students expect instant gratification, but students often have difficulty recognizing progress when it is not immediate. Consider the following two perspectives: a child will never notice that they are growing taller, yet a grandparent who sees that child only twice a year is likely to lament how fast that child is growing! Without a way to demonstrate musical growth, students may feel like their progress has stalled. Detailed records allow teachers to track student progress, which should be regularly shared with students. With such records, Alex and Eli might have been able to co-construct a more meaningful approach with manageable goals that were valued by both teacher and student.

> *We have presented several alternatives to this narrative.*
>
> *What other factors may have contributed to a more positive experience for Eli?*

Scenario 1.2: Annual Evaluation

Conny is a first-year orchestra teacher in a small rural school district. She grew up in a neighboring town, and was very excited to have a job so close to home. Her teaching load included two orchestras (one at the middle school and one at the high school), pull-out lessons, and one section of middle school general music. She felt her students were making excellent progress, and was already thinking about how to expand the curriculum for next year.

In mid-April, Conny scheduled her Annual Evaluation with the principal. She was a little nervous, but understood these evaluations were a normal part of the job. The principal, a 20-year veteran teacher-turned-administrator, had a reputation for being supportive – but blunt. Conny had looked through her evidence binder the night before, and felt prepared. She was thankful her mentor teacher had encouraged her to collect samples of student work, formative and summative assessments, documentation of professional development, and concert programs to prepare for this meeting!

For the majority of the meeting, Conny's principal reviewed the results from formal observations. She was generally pleased with how well Conny had fit into the school community, her classroom management, organization, and rapport with students, but she expressed some concerns with Conny's instructional choices. "The previous teacher used to take the high school orchestra to the string orchestra state music festival." "In your second observation, you divided the group into smaller sections. This seemed rather chaotic." "I appreciate your originality – the composing project is a nice idea – but I think you should really focus your energy on more exciting concerts."

Conny left the meeting feeling very uncertain about her teaching ability and how to proceed. She thought to herself, "Am I doing this all wrong?"

> *How would you feel in this situation?*
>
> *How would you respond to this principal, if you were the teacher in this narrative?*

Reflection

There are several embedded assumptions in this scenario (see Chapter 2). Bourdieu's concept of *habitus* (refer to Scenario 1.1) may help to explain the structure in which this scenario exists. Roger Mantie and Brent Talbot summarized the inherent difficulty of introducing elements of change into existing models of music education:

> Efforts to recognize and critique (let alone change!) the habits of the status quo are enormously difficult because the flywheel of the American music teacher education system is so monolithic in its historically-produced weight and momentum that it (a) serves to blind us from alternatives, and (b) it polices action so effectively that contrarian voices are often kept in isolation so they cannot "act." — Mantie & Talbot[7]

Change is difficult.
Researchers have provided numerous reasons why change is difficult in educational settings.[8] The principal in this scenario alluded to one such reason – perhaps subconsciously – when she referenced the "previous teacher." Conny can either view this conflict as an insurmountable obstacle, or as an opportunity to have a meaningful conversation with her principal. In this situation, we would encourage Conny to take the following steps: reflect, discuss, and revise.

Reflect.
Conny should try to objectively consider her principal's feedback and realize they both have the students' best interests in mind, though she and Conny may have different opinions of what that looks like. Conny should allow herself time to experience emotions including doubt and frustration. Conny should also maintain a growth mindset,[9] and view this meeting as an opportunity to discuss the best possible learning experiences for her students, address the

principal's concerns, and revise her practice. She might construct an email to her principal:

> "Thank you for your feedback. You've given me a lot to think about, and I would like to continue this conversation. Would you have time to meet with me again next week, after I have had time to reflect on our meeting?"

Discuss.

Assuming the principal is amenable to another meeting, Conny will need to prepare for the meeting. Conny should begin by thanking the principal for her time. She should then articulate her purpose for requesting a meeting. This will help keep the atmosphere professional, relaxed, and calm, and ensure that both parties are working toward the best student experience.

Here is one possible approach Conny might take:

> "Thank you for meeting with me. I've given a lot of thought to the concerns you raised, and would like your feedback on my ideas."

The principal is unlikely to perceive this approach as defensive, and gives Conny the opportunity to demonstrate that she is a thoughtful and reflective teacher. Conny should plan to address the principal's concerns by restating them, providing evidence and rationale, and offering potential solutions. This approach is likely to facilitate a healthy and productive meeting.

Conny could use this opportunity to demonstrate that she borrowed and adopted curricular ideas from other teachers (cross-disciplinary, within the music department, and from the previous teacher whom she replaced), gotten to know her students' musical interests and aspirations, set expectations that are based on national and state music learning standards, and demonstrated musical growth through detailed record keeping. These concepts are taken from the general and music-specific ideas offered in the beginning of this chapter. Conny might address the composition project as follows:

> "You mentioned the composition project was a nice idea, but it seems like you feel that might get in the way of providing exciting concerts. I included that project for several reasons. I am personally really passionate about composing, the National Standards for Music Education call for all students to create music, and I wanted to give the students the opportunity to develop their own musical voice. However, several students mentioned they would have liked to play something 'more contemporary' in their concert evaluations. Next year, I'd like to teach a popular song by ear, have students compose an arrangement for the ensemble, and then have them perform this on the concert. I think this might be a better way to meet both of our expectations for the students. What do you think?"

Revise.

After the meeting, Conny will have a better understanding of her principal's expectations and will be in a better position to critically reflect on her practice. Ideally, this meeting will allow Conny and her principal to collaborate and develop a solution. Through critical reflection and an open-minded approach, Conny will be able to revise and refine her curriculum for the following year. Ultimately, Conny can uphold her educational priorities while her philosophy continues to evolve.

> *We offered one approach Conny might have taken.*
>
> *How else might she have reacted, and what are the possible outcomes?*
>
> *What other general or music-specific advice might help Conny's situation?*

Summary

In the beginning of this chapter, we shared some common advice you are likely to hear as you transition from pre-service to in-service music teacher. Some are general words of wisdom, and some will be music-specific. Here they are, again:

General Ideas	*Music-Specific Ideas*
- Be yourself. - Set expectations. - Learn your students' names. - Learn your students' stories. - Borrow ideas from other teachers. - Be a reflective practitioner. - Develop an organizational strategy. - Connect with support staff.	- Uncover your students' musical interests and goals. - Share your passions. - Be mindful when defining "quality" music. - Identify curricular stakeholders. - Maintain detailed records. - Be a music maker.

Chapter 2

Unpacking Assumptions

All music teachers enter the profession with ideas about what is best for students. These ideas are commonly shaped by what they learned in college (explicitly-transmitted pedagogical knowledge) and the teaching practices they observed as students (implicitly-acquired learning experiences). These factors contribute to a personal philosophy of teaching—which is extremely important for teachers to develop! However, it is also important to critically evaluate the assumptions that shape our personal philosophies. In this chapter, we will identify and discuss some of the benefits and pitfalls of established traditions in music teaching and learning.

Early-career music teachers commonly emulate the teaching practices they received as young students. As Randall Allsup notes, "persons who come to and from replicas of these historic programs are individuals submerged by the rules of its practice and are thus likely to embody class situations that are bound by its discourses."[1] Exposure to varied pedagogical ideas in college may not provide a sufficient catalyst to fundamentally change these deeply ingrained practices. Bourdieu described his concept of *habitus* as the internalizing structures of society and culture, "inscribed in the body of the biological individual."[2] Habitus provides an appropriate lens through which to view the conflict between old and new; between tradition and innovation. Through reflective praxis, music teachers can learn to recognize habitus and make informed decisions regarding curriculum and instruction. It is impossible for pre-service music teachers to fully prepare for every possible K–12 teaching experience, so it is critically important for early career music teachers to practice reflexivity.[3]

Reflective music teachers work hard to meet the needs of their students and expectations of their stakeholders. Every decision to *include* an activity means that other activities are *excluded*. Connelly and Clandinin refer to this concept as the *null curriculum*. Closely related is their idea of a *hidden curriculum*, which serves to perpetuate "a hierarchical social structure that benefits some at the expense of others."[4] It is important for music teachers to recognize common misconceptions embedded within our profession so we may make more informed curricular decisions.

Common Misconceptions

Misconception #1:
There is only one way to define excellence.
On the contrary, excellence is a process. Your perception of excellence may differ from your predecessor, supervisor, colleagues, and students. Along with your students—and other curricular stakeholders—you must establish the standards for defining excellence. If you set parameters that allow your students to realize success, they are more likely to feel proud of their accomplishments. Peter Boonshaft suggests even seemingly insignificant moments have the potential to set off a chain reaction leading to powerful experiences.[5] You must always strive for excellence, and encourage your students to do the same.

Misconception #2:
You must focus on historically-celebrated composers.
Traditionally, Western classical music has favored white, male composers. You can broaden this understanding and encourage exploration and discovery of new interests by highlighting diverse cultural forms through the music you teach. Students develop perceptions of who can become musically educated, talented, and celebrated through the music and skills they learn. Encourage students to explore music written by a diverse group of composers and show them everyone can learn and make music.

> In an analysis of 120 different American orchestras during the 2019-20 Orchestra Season, the Institute for Composer Diversity found there were more performances of works by Beethoven (n = 434, 10.5%), than by all female composers combined (n = 309, 8%), or by diverse racial, ethnic, and cultural heritages (n = 224, 6%).[6]

Misconception #3:
Classical ensembles require classical repertoire.
Teachers often prioritize classical music over popular music in ensembles, but forget that classical music was popular music when it was first performed! Include popular music in your classroom to teach important concepts and skills. You may increase student motivation, enrollment, and overall joy of learning by including music your students find relevant and relatable.

Misconception #4:
Performances should maintain established traditions.
A concert performance or recital program that includes only classical music and method book excerpts may exclude the interests of students wanting to learn music from other genres such as pop, rock, jazz, etc. Inviting community musicians to perform, starting a concert tradition in a community venue, or integrating student compositions may serve to showcase non-traditional elements of your curriculum and better involve the community.

Misconception #5:
Trust the way it's always been done.
Tradition requires as much justification as innovation. If you choose to perpetuate a tradition, you should also be able to justify this decision. Similarly, if you attempt to change a longstanding practice, you should have a reason for doing so. The way it's always been done may not still be the best approach for the current situation.

Misconception #6:
Students benefit most from private lessons.
Private lesson teachers play an important role and have the unique opportunity to provide one-on-one, individualized attention to each student. However, students more naturally acquire musicianship skills in group settings and/or around people of their own age.[7] Private studio teachers should encourage regular studio classes or group lessons to diversify the learning environment.

Misconception #7:
Reading music should be the highest priority.
Reading, writing, composing, arranging, and improvising are all part of a well-rounded music education.[8] Researchers have repeatedly shown that infants (less than one year old) produce and differentiate between speech-like and musical vocalizations—long before they develop the ability to read or write.[9] Playing by ear, improvising, and composing are some of the earliest and most uniquely human inclinations! We will explore the importance of creative musical activities in music instruction more deeply in Chapter 5. However, whether or not you consider yourself a competent composer or improviser, you are certainly equipped to offer feedback about the music students learn by ear or create themselves.

Misconception #8:
There's not enough time to ignore technique.
Music teachers commonly believe that, after teaching students to read music notation, teaching technique is the most important

facet of their jobs. As such, music teachers are likely to assume they need to invest a significant amount of time teaching technical skills. This is especially true for private instruction, where teachers typically instruct one student at a time on their primary instrument and can help fine tune techniques that others may not catch. While there certainly is an air of truth to this, it is important to provide a tailored musical experience. Remember: technique should aid musicianship, not the other way around.

Scenarios

In this section, we offer three scenarios for you to consider. After each scenario, we unpack some of the inherent assumptions embedded in each story and reflect on the possible consequences. Following each reflection, we offer additional questions for you to consider. As an exercise, imagine how you would respond if confronted with similar situations.

The first scenario is about Holly, a first-year teacher who is taking over a well-respected middle school band program. The second scenario tells the story of a private lesson teacher named David, who has developed a piano studio that became important to the community. In the third scenario, Susan is a third-year adjunct cello professor who must navigate the challenges of changing job responsibilities.

Scenario 2.1: First-Year Band Director

Holly is a first-year middle school band director in an affluent school system. Before the start of the school year, she attended the first music department meeting with all the band directors from the district. They quickly welcomed her to the district and informed her that she landed a great job! At the meeting, Holly learned the school board decided to name the new music wing after her predecessor, John Marshall, when he retired. The music department supervisor referred to Mr. Marshall as "a legend" who was single-handedly responsible for the excellence of the band program. Holly's new colleagues said she was lucky to have been named as his replacement, especially as a first-year teacher. She saw the trophies displayed on the shelves in the band room and felt she had big shoes to fill.

As the meeting continued, the music supervisor reviewed the levels of support for music education in the school district and surrounding community. The Parent-Teacher Association publicized private lesson programs and summer music camps, the Board of Education approved the purchase of new marching uniforms, the district had agreed to host a county-wide band festival and corresponding honor band for the third consecutive year, and there was a music store representative (a "road rep," Holly learned) who had already distributed instrument rental information to all elementary schools. The supervisor announced he arranged to fly in a renowned conductor to direct a commissioned piece with this year's honor band, and ended the meeting by saying this year was going to be "the best one yet." Holly left the meeting feeling incredibly fortunate to have inherited a program that already seemed to run like a well-oiled machine.

That afternoon, back at her school, Holly finally got the keys to her new band room. She began taking inventory of instruments, walking through the auditorium, and printing class rosters. Before she left for the day, she set up chairs and stands, copied some warm-ups, scheduled concert dates and after-school rehearsals, and even restrung the French horn she found sitting in the back corner of the room. Feeling a big sense of accomplishment, she thought to herself "Wow. Those other band directors were right: I really am lucky to be here!"

Reflection

This scenario is loaded with assumptions about curriculum, professional relationships, implications for how and what to teach, and exclusionary teaching practices. For example, Holly might reasonably assume that in order to live up to the reputation of her predecessor, she has to continue to win trophies. This would require her to enter her ensembles into a competition, which is likely to influence her repertoire and lesson planning. Did the word "lucky" stick out to you when reading this scenario? To imply that Holly is "lucky" to have this job undermines her professionalism and qualifications, and suggests that she didn't actually *earn* the job! In this scenario, Holly may certainly feel fortunate to have earned this job, but she must be careful to avoid several misconceptions:

Misconception #1:
You must live up to the reputation of your predecessor.
While it may be helpful for Holly to understand and consider the environment in place before she was hired, she should not feel pressured to carry on her predecessor's legacy; she was hired for the value that she brought to the position. Stephen Nachmanovitch describes this as a "fear of ghosts:"

> Deviation from the true self often arises from comparison with or envy of the idealized other… Brahms couldn't finish his first symphony for twenty-two years because he had a monkey on his back called Beethoven… It's great to sit on the shoulders of giants, but don't let the giants sit on *your* shoulders! There's no room for their legs to dangle.[10]

Misconception #2:
You must emulate veteran teachers.
Navigating the social dynamics and power structures of a public school teaching position can be tricky. Veteran teachers serve many roles. Music teachers should not feel obligated to impress a colleague, unless the colleague serves in an evaluatory capacity. As

we mentioned in Chapter 1, veteran teachers are bound to provide valuable information, and developing productive relationships with veteran teachers can strengthen the sense of community among colleagues. While veteran teachers are often excellent resources and positive support systems, they should not dictate curriculum.

Misconception #3:
You must adhere to established definitions of excellence.
With time, Holly is likely to develop the experience and confidence to shape the culture of her own program. As long as she doesn't feel pressured to sacrifice her teaching philosophy or principles, Holly may well choose to adopt and adapt ideas from her predecessor. But, as we said before, perceptions of excellence may differ between early-career music teachers and their predecessors, supervisors, colleagues, and students. No one definition is necessarily better than another, but changing long-established and firmly-held definitions of excellence takes time. Major change doesn't happen in just one year—let alone overnight!

> *Can you identify elements of the hidden or null curriculum?*
>
> *What other assumptions exist in this scenario?*
>
> *What else might Holly consider in her position?*

Other Considerations

Successful band programs are often defined by the number of students in the program. Directors of such programs may boast about students who are obedient, follow directions, show loyalty to the band program, and are always available to attend extra rehearsals and extracurricular events. We encourage teachers to reflect on common practices that may undervalue or exclude certain populations. Those who develop the habit of asking critical questions (like the ones below) might foster a more inclusive climate.

- What accommodations exist for students with physical disabilities in a traditional band program?
- How does repertoire dictate ensemble instrumentation?
- How do teacher expectations about "appropriate" behavior and "important" music skills influence the curriculum?
- What is the process for selecting music to perform, and how does this music represent the musical identities of this particular group of students?
- By picking and rehearsing concert music early, how much time is devoted to other learning standards (e.g., composing, arranging, or improvising)?
- How do private lessons, after-school rehearsals, summer music camps, band festivals, instrument rentals, fundraisers, and uniforms contribute to the music program? To what extent do they favor or marginalize students?

Scenario 2.2: Neighborhood Private Lesson Teacher

Throughout high school, David was known for his prodigious sight-reading and performance skills. He was fortunate to have a private piano teacher who taught him to read music from an early age, and fully immersed him in the classical piano tradition. While David loved piano, he never planned to pursue piano as a profession. In college, David majored in economics and landed a job as a financial advisor for a respectable firm where he had worked for the past 10 years.

David still loved to play piano. His job at the financial firm allowed him to teach in-home piano lessons during the evening and on weekends, and he performed regularly at an assisted living facility. Over the last five years, David developed a studio so large he had to recruit other respected classical pianists to help with the teaching load, organize recitals, and manage the weekly teaching schedule and accounts. His lesson program was viewed throughout the community as reputable and affordable.

In a typical lesson, David included scales, arpeggios, a little bit of music theory, and a solo piece for the annual recital. His students typically excelled at note and rhythm reading skills. David structured his program so that beginning students learned the layout of the piano and simple melodic note reading, and advanced students learned Bach inventions, Scarlatti etudes, and Chopin polonaises. David and his staff focused on a healthy balance of sight-reading, technique, and classical repertoire — the hallmarks of any good piano program. On occasion, typically in the weeks following a recital, David would pull out a book of pop favorites for students to sight-read. The students always loved this activity, particularly since they rarely had time for "extras" like this.

Every student performed in the spring recital, which was held at the local church. This year, the place was packed — standing room only in the back of the sanctuary! Students performed solo classical pieces and duets, some with notation and some from memory. Beginning students performed pieces from their method books. As the recital continued, the performances grew more impressive. Finally, the most accomplished student gave a rousing rendition of Liszt's *Hungarian Rhapsody* that earned a standing ovation. Every student worked hard to prepare for this event, and David was proud that every student had shown demonstrable progress. David was very grateful for his staff — all of their planning and preparation had truly paid off.

Reflection

The neighborhood piano teacher is often a staple of the musical community who might teach hundreds of students over the course of their career. These educators provide meaningful music experiences for students of all ages who want to learn to play an instrument not commonly taught in school settings. However, it is important to recognize the assumptions embedded in private lesson settings.

Here are three misconceptions David might have had when creating and organizing his piano studio:

Misconception #1:
The focus of lessons is to prepare for the performance.
Learning repertoire is a great way to build context for the scales, arpeggios, and other skills drilled in lessons. When music teachers focus exclusively on the performance product as the vehicle for skill development, they neglect students' natural curiosity and exploration. The process of musical play provides many valuable learning opportunities, and is a worthy end in itself.

Misconception #2:
Private studios should prioritize formal performances.
Even though David allowed students to sight-read pop music after recitals, he might consider integrating other styles of music throughout the regular curriculum. David could consider programming contemporary music on a recital program, or allowing students to jam on a regular basis and in formal concert settings. Although many popular music transcriptions and arrangements are over-simplified to reach a broader audience, quality arrangements provide the same opportunities as the classics to teach technical skills.

Misconception #3:
Teachers determine what knowledge is most worth knowing.
Private studios often have a unique perspective on their community. While school classrooms and community groups often include

students of similar ages, abilities, and interests, private studios cater to a broader population with various reasons for pursuing private lessons. Teachers must consider what material is the most relevant to the student. Gouzouasis & Ryu wrote, "What a piano teacher may think is meaningful in terms of music learning may be overshadowed by something 'other' than what we typically consider as music learning."[11]

> *If you were to design your own private studio, what learning behaviors would you prioritize?*

Other Considerations

Private music studios are often pillars in a community. Although this scenario is specific to a private piano studio, it also applies directly to community music school teachers. While developing the structure for a studio, consider the following:

- What discussions will you have with students and their parents about your plan for what students will learn? What expectations do parents have from you? What do your students expect to learn from studying with you?

- What specific music skills (e.g., sight-reading, improvisation, composition, arranging) should you prioritize? What will your students be able to do when they leave your studio?

- Do your students have music teachers outside of your studio? Do your students make music in school or elsewhere in the community?

- How much choice will you afford your students in deciding what and how they will learn?

- What local school music teachers might you contact? How can you support school music learning?

Scenario 2.3: Adjunct Cello Professor

In college, Susan studied music education and cello performance, maintaining high performance standards on her primary instrument. She practiced diligently and performed regularly with various musicians around town. Her most influential teachers were experts at their instrument, performed constantly, and loved teaching. Not surprisingly, Susan also valued a high level of performance skill. She believed this was a necessary component of highly successful teachers, and was eager to teach students to love cello as much as she did. Her goal was always to become a collegiate cello professor. She dreamed of a scenario in which she would likely be able to teach and perform simultaneously.

After graduating from college, Susan applied to a local university and—to her excitement and surprise—earned her first teaching job as an adjunct professor. She began teaching with great enthusiasm for her studio, tirelessly recruiting students and earning the respect of her colleagues. Near the end of her first year, the violin professor had to leave abruptly for health reasons. The department chair asked Susan to cover some violin lessons because the university was unable to hire a replacement in time. Despite her reservations and inexperience teaching upper strings students, she reluctantly accepted his request. It *was* her first year teaching, and she did not want to offend the department chair.

During the next two years, Susan's teaching load became split between low and high strings. Some semesters, the bulk of her studio was violinists. Though she had voiced her concerns to several colleagues, she felt they didn't really understand or appreciate her position. Susan was receiving a modest stipend for teaching over her contractual workload, but had trouble finding time to practice or perform as much anymore. Now, in her third year at this university, Susan felt as though the university had given up on replacing the violin professor. Eventually, Susan started to wonder how long she could continue along this path without burning out. She recalled the enthusiasm she felt at the beginning of her career and thought, "How do I return to that level of joy in teaching again?"

Reflection

The two primary sources of Susan's frustration seems to be changing job conditions and a perceived lack of support. Teachers are commonly asked to teach outside their immediate area of expertise, and can still provide extraordinary musical experiences with their existing musicianship and teaching skills. If Susan expected to teach her primary instrument forever, any deviation from this would likely lead to disappointment and dissatisfaction.

Teachers who feel supported by their colleagues may be better equipped to problem-solve job-related issues.[12] Susan may have had a better reaction from her colleagues if she expressed her feelings honestly and without complaining. If Susan were to reframe her complaints as concerns, with the intent of developing a solution, her colleagues may feel more comfortable offering advice.

As with the previous scenarios, we would like to highlight some assumptions that led Susan to her current situation:

Misconception #1:
Job descriptions should not change.
Change is hard. Teachers must adapt to meet the needs of changing circumstances. In this scenario, Susan will need to decide if she can adapt to fit the current demands of her job, or if she should start to look elsewhere for a more suitable position. Teachers who feel "stuck," underappreciated, or burned out are not in a position to effectively care for their students. Nobody should feel like they have to "deal with" their job—once this happens, something needs to change!

Misconception #2:
Teachers determine who and what to teach.
Teachers should be able to influence who and what they teach, but there are many other factors (e.g. financial considerations, accreditation requirements, physical space restraints, educational policy) that affect these decisions. Sometimes, these external factors can result in feelings of anxiety and frustration. It is normal to feel unprepared or overwhelmed on occasion, but viewing challenges as opportunities for growth may yield a more positive experience—for both teachers and students.

> *How would you advocate for change if you were Susan?*
>
> *Have you been in a similar situation?*
> *How did you react?*

Other Considerations

Contingent faculty comprise a significant portion of collegiate teaching positions. Nearly two-thirds of postsecondary appointments are non-tenure track or part-time faculty.[13] Recent college graduates recruited to fill these vacancies must remember there is more to a music career than simply teaching music. It is perfectly normal (and healthy!) to consider such factors as income, retirement, health care, cost of living, and family responsibilities. Remember, your first job does not have to be your forever job. If circumstances change, consider the following questions when determining how to respond:

- What do you still love about your job?
- What is within your power to change?
- Which elements are you willing to accept?
- Is this job still a good fit for you?

These may be difficult questions to ponder, but your time and happiness are absolutely worth it! Mitchell Robinson offers some practical words of wisdom:

> As teachers, we need to stop romanticizing our profession... We can also stop using hackneyed phrases such as 'Teaching. I'm not in it for the income; I'm in it for the outcomes,' or other meme-worthy sayings that imply that teachers don't need to be compensated fairly, or don't require adequate benefit packages, like health care insurance and pensions.[14]

In retrospect, Susan might have politely asked her department chair for some time to consider his request. This would have given her time to construct a response that allowed her to voice her reluctance and state her concerns in a respectful, professional manner. Given her present situation in this scenario, Susan has several options to regain control of her career. She can either (a) try to improve her situation by changing her mindset (remember the importance of developing a growth mindset, referred to in Chapter 1), (b) share her concerns with the department chair, or (c) give herself permission to look for another job. If we were able to counsel Susan in this scenario, we would ask the following questions:

- What types of musical experiences *can* you provide your upper string students during their lessons?

- How might you develop your students' musical independence, and thereby transcend your perceived limitations?

- Have you tried modeling musical examples on your primary instrument? How might this change your teaching strategies?

- What online resources exist (YouTube videos, blog posts, research forums, etc.) that might help you grow as a teacher? What online resources might provide important supplemental information to your students?

- Have you discussed your concerns with your department chair? He may not even realize that you are unhappy with your current situation.

- What specific elements of your job would you like to change? Can you provide a rationale and offer suggestions for making these changes? If you can provide your department chair with a rationale and a proposed solution, he may be able to advocate for you more effectively.

- What does your ideal job look like? Would it be worth considering a job change? What are you willing to give up, and what do you hope to gain?

Summary

By asking tough questions like the ones above, teachers reconsider massive and important issues surrounding our profession. Making changes in the name of inclusion will allow teachers to better connect with students, provide relevant instruction, and increase student motivation.

In summary, here is a list of the assumptions we included at the beginning of the chapter for your reference:

- There is only one way to define excellence.
- You must focus on historically celebrated composers.
- Classical ensembles require classical repertoire.
- Performances should maintain established standards.
- Trust the way it's always been done.
- Students benefit most from private lessons.
- Reading music should be the highest priority.
- There's not enough time to ignore technique.

Chapter 3

Critical Self-Reflection

Scenario 3.1: "Got a minute?"

This scenario recounts a real conversation I (Erik) had with a former student who had just finished her first year teaching public school music.

I had just finished my spring concert season, and my high school students were working on a composition project to end the year. Late-spring in upstate New York is a beautiful time of year, and everybody was getting excited for the end of the school year. It was around this time that I received an email from a former student. The subject: "Got a minute?"

As a high school music teacher, I often have the opportunity to work closely with students for four consecutive years. Addie (a pseudonym) and I arrived at the high school in the same year—Addie as a freshman, and I as a third-year teacher who had just changed jobs. Five years after high school, Addie graduated college with a dual degree in music performance and education.

Though I hadn't heard from Addie in awhile, her email provided a welcome relief from the growing list of to-do items mounting in my inbox. (Admittedly, my first thoughts were: "Wait… wasn't she *just* in 9th grade? Where did the time go?!!") In her email, Addie explained she had nearly finished her first year teaching elementary instrumental music and was looking for some advice. We planned to talk over lunch once the school year ended.

When we met at the end of June, Addie enthusiastically told me all about her first year. She felt she had made some important changes in her program, and was excited about the possibilities of her new music department. At the same time, Addie was overwhelmed with this new level of responsibility. In her words, "I just want to give my students the best musical experience possible, but there's SO MUCH to think about!" Addie asked specific questions about selecting instructional resources, my pedagogy and philosophy, financing her program, and professional development opportunities. She also wanted to know how I motivated students to practice, how I connected with the community, and how I supported students who struggled while still challenging the students who excelled.

I found that the answers she was seeking could only be found through reflective dialogue. To help her work through these important questions, I responded with even bigger questions: "What went well this past year, and why? What can you change for next year, and what can wait? What other resources or information do you need to better align your practice with your goals and objectives?" After several hours of questions, enthusiastic debate, and more questions, we eventually concluded: "There are no answers!"

Reflection

While the first few years of teaching provide excellent context for reflection, it is important to continue reflecting throughout your entire career. As you adapt your teaching practices, make sure to plan innovation with students in mind and stay informed about best teaching practices. Remember, progress takes time, so be patient while working through new ideas.

Using Scenario 3.1 as a framework for the rest of this chapter, we urge you to continuously reflect on your successes and challenges and remain connected to the larger community of professional music teachers through professional development and student-centered innovation.

> *How would you answer these questions Erik posed to Addie?*
> - *What went well this past year, and why?*
> - *What can you change for next year, and what can wait?*
> - *What else can you do to help you align your practice with your philosophy?*

Reflecting on Successes and Challenges

Consider the first question Erik asked Addie: "What went well this past year, and why?" The emotions of the early part of a teacher's career tend to generate a lot of in-the-moment reflection. It is important to capture your emotions while teaching, as you will be able to recall "all the feels" without the fading effect of time. Time, however, can be a great mediator. You will experience a wide range of emotions as an early-career music teacher—these emotions mediate your perceptions of success and failure. When we experience emotions, they tend to gravitate toward the extremes; successes seem almost magical, and challenges may feel unbearable. By reflecting on your successes and challenges over time, you are engaging in a process of reflection at a metalevel. The successes are better connected to reality, and the challenges seem more manageable.

We offer two strategies to help track these thoughts and emotions, and use them to enact meaningful change in your specific learning situation: keep a journal and reflect annually.

Keep a journal.
If you haven't already, develop a habit of recording your thoughts and ideas as you reflect on your teaching experiences. You might consider a small notebook, app, or a web-based platform you can access anytime or anywhere an idea strikes you. After each major event, make time to reflect on your successes and challenges—but don't get discouraged! Instead, purposefully reflect on how your actions support the needs of your students. Remember, positive relationships are a prerequisite to change. Significant changes require significant time. As you journal and reflect, consider how each change may shape your program and your identity as a teacher.

Solicit feedback from students.
In Chapter 1, we identified a variety of stakeholders—including administrators, colleagues, students and parents—who might provide curricular input. Since administrators and colleagues may not always be available to visit your classroom, your primary feedback may be candid responses from your students. Incorporate journal entry ideas and student feedback when crafting new lessons and assessments. You may be able to intuit student opinions by reading body language, but a far more effective practice might be to gather direct feedback through regular surveys. Through careful consideration of students' needs, you can ensure your decisions prioritize students' interests.

Reflect annually.
"What went well this semester? …this month? …this unit? …this week? …today?!" You can reframe the temporality of these questions , but it may be easiest to work through them at the end of each school year. "Zoom out" of the day-to-day, and think about your decisions from a wider lens. Developing these reflective habits is paramount to building a successful career. We have included a Year-End Reflection Worksheet for you to use, duplicate, adapt, and share.

Innovate with Student Learning in Mind

In Scenario 3.1, Erik encouraged Addie to prioritize changes: "What can you change for next year, and what can wait?"

Your experiences as a musician and teacher should guide your planning and teaching, but not dictate completely what your students learn. After all, you learned music at a different time. While there may be some aspects of music you believe every musician should know, remember you do not need to replicate every experience you had. As you plan for each year, consider how well you are connecting to students, colleagues, and community members. Social media, podcasts, or blog posts could showcase less visible aspects of your class. While concerts highlight the collective success of an ensemble's hard work, these other platforms could feature students learning to compose, improvise, arrange, play other instruments, produce, etc. Setting up these platforms can also help you stay committed to reflective and innovative practices. Most importantly, whenever you innovate, consider how students will benefit and how your professional relationship with them comes into play.

Year-End Reflection Worksheet

List FIVE successes; things that went well:

List THREE things that could have gone better:

What might you do differently if given a second chance?

List TWO new ideas/concepts you'd like to try next year and when/how that might fit into your existing curriculum:

Connect with students.
Teachers have differing philosophies about connecting with their students. Some teachers maintain strictly musical relationships; others focus on developing musical relationships that also include personal connections. Your approach to making connections will likely vary by student. One effective way to navigate this process is to reflect on your relationships with former teachers. What made you feel comfortable, appreciated, or appropriately challenged in the learning process? What type of teacher did you best learn from? Connect with? Reflecting on your past experiences reminds you of what it's like to be a student. The more you think about your connection style, the more effectively you can innovate with students in mind.

Reflect even when no one's watching.
While you may be required to strictly adhere to certain policies and meet specific guidelines, you may also have a lot of autonomy in your job—perhaps more than you realize. In some jobs, you may be required to produce some results like performance ratings, retention rates, etc., but have freedom to achieve these in any way you choose. For example, while earning certain scores at adjudicated events may be widely valued by your community, your rehearsal technique, pacing, and choices about what skills you teach may be less scrutinized. This freedom comes with great responsibility and an even greater need to reflect and revise teaching practices with students in mind.

Analyze and evaluate how much time you spend on certain class activities. If classes typically consist of a warm-up followed by group or sectional rehearsals, you could use some of that time for exploratory and creative projects. You might also point out compositional techniques used in a piece of concert repertoire and/or ask students to create their own piece using those same techniques. (See Chapter 6 for more project ideas.) Restructuring class time allows you to teach how structural elements—harmony, layering, balance, timbre—function in composition and performance.

In addition to reallocating class time, you may also have the freedom to reformat traditional events like concerts and festivals. These events have tremendous potential for engaging the community and showing how your classes meet students' needs. Achieving success in performance feels wonderful, and provides an opportunity to think about ways to increase inclusion. Have students demonstrate various skills learned in your class in a performance setting. You could facilitate exhibition stations where students show how they have learned to compose, improvise, arrange, play other instruments, produce, etc. By adapting your class time and events, you increase the quality of instruction and show commitment to student learning and community values.

> *What other practices can you change to include, engage, and empower more students more deeply?*

Staying Informed

Erik also asked Addie: "What other resources or information do you need to better align your practice with your goals and objectives?"

This is fundamentally a question about personal learning and professional growth. As you reflect on your experiences and plan for innovation, you will need additional tools to help you meet your goals and objectives. Learn how to locate and use academic research. Identify relevant and meaningful professional development opportunities. Locate resources that will help you continue learning. Although these may not seem immediately relevant at the very beginning of your career, your continued success as a reflective music teacher is contingent upon your continued ability to grow musically and pedagogically.

Forty-seven states currently require continued professional development. (Only California, New Jersey, and Rhode Island have not adopted state-wide professional development for teaching licensure at the time of publication.[1] Individual school districts in these states may have their own specific requirements.) Whether or not you are required to complete professional development—and even if you have already completed the required amount—attending conferences, workshops, and clinics provide excellent opportunities to learn new ideas and ways of thinking, and allow you to remain connected to current research, other music teachers, and best practices.

You may have access to financial support for engaging in professional development. Your employer may allocate funding or time for this purpose. Local colleges may offer discounts to area teachers to audit a course or attend a workshop. County or state music educator associations (MEAs) may sponsor early-career teachers to attend conferences. Another important part of attending conferences, workshops, and clinics is making connections and collaborating with other teachers.

Related Resources

One challenge with attending professional development workshops, conferences, and clinics is that they only occur on specific dates and in set locations. There are several online platforms that allow you to continue learning at more convenient times and places. Some are free and some require a paid subscription. You may have access to these resources through your employer, local library, through a membership in the National Association for Music Education (NAfME), or possibly as an alumni privilege through your college institution. Here are a few online platforms to explore:

Google Scholar (scholar.google.com)
Google Scholar provides a way to search for scholarly literature. You can search across many disciplines and sources—articles, theses, books, abstracts and court opinions—from academic publishers, professional societies, online repositories, universities and other websites.[2]

Education Resources Information Center (eric.ed.gov)
ERIC is a digital library of education research and information that provides access to bibliographic records of journal and non-journal literature from 1966 to the present. ERIC's mission is to provide a comprehensive, easy-to-use, searchable Internet-based bibliographic and full-text database of education research and information for educators, researchers, and the general public.[3]

JSTOR (jstor.org)
JSTOR is another digital library that provides access to more than 12 million academic journal articles, books, and primary sources in 75 disciplines. These collections are integrated on one platform that allows users to access these resources through an institutional or individual account.[4]

ProQuest (proquest.com)
ProQuest provides information and services to academic, corporate, government, school and public libraries, as well as professional researchers. It also enables acquisition, management, and discovery of information collections. ProQuest strives to increase the productivity of students, scholars, professionals and the libraries that serve them by providing innovative information content and technologies.[5]

Journals and Magazines

Academic journals and practitioner magazines allow music teachers to stay connected to research and best practices. Academic journals are geared toward original research, and practitioner magazines offer a forum for scholars to share practical applications of teaching strategies. Journals and magazines are both valuable, but serve very different purposes. Access to both may be included through your state music educators association.

Music Education Journals

Most music journals aim to publish original research conducted by one or more individuals. Before a researcher can conduct a study on human subjects, they must submit a proposal to an Institutional Review Board (IRB). The IRB will ensure that research activities are ethical, objective, and that the subjects of the research study are protected. In order for research to be published, authors must submit an article to the editor of a journal. The editor typically sends the article to three reviewers after ensuring the author can not be identified in the manuscript (this is called a blind-review). These reviewers are usually experts in the research topic, and must approve that the research study adheres to rigorous standards of scholarship. As such, research articles have been thoroughly vetted for accuracy and objectivity.

If you have never read a research article, it may help to understand how they are formatted. Most music journals use the American Psychological Association (APA) formatting. Citations appear in text using an (Author, Date, page number) format. Most research articles begin with an Abstract, which is a brief summary of the whole paper. Start here to get an overview of the rest of the article. The Introduction establishes the context for study and often includes a comprehensive review of related research. At the end of the Introduction, authors often include the Purpose Statement and Research Questions. A Methodology section generally comes next, in which the author describes the procedures used to conduct the study. In the Results section, the author shares the results of the study. In a quantitative study, this generally includes a lot of statistics; qualitative studies often provide evidence of findings that support the development of themes. Following the Results section, the Discussion section usually describes how the results answer the research questions guiding the study. Finally, the Conclusion summarizes the research, offers suggestions for future research, and describes how the research contributes to the field of music research.

You can access most research journals online through one of the websites listed previously in this chapter. We have included a list of some popular music education journals. This list is not comprehensive, and we encourage you to use these as a point of departure.

- Bulletin of the Council for Research in Music Education
- International Journal of Music Education
- Journal of Historical Research in Music Education
- Journal of Research in Music Education
- Journal of Music Teacher Education
- Music Education Research
- Music Perception
- Research Studies in Music Education
- Update: Applications of Research in Music Education

One strategy for reading these articles is to start with the Abstract to get a general idea of the paper, then skip to the end of the Introduction section. After finding the purpose statement, you could skip to the Discussion or Conclusion section to read the results. If you want to know more details, dig in to the Methodology and Results sections for more specific information.

Magazines
Practitioner magazines offer resources for new teaching ideas. Although magazines have an editor who reviews every submission, not all magazine articles are subject to a rigorous blind-review process by a panel of experts. However, magazine contributors often include collegiate music students, practicing music teachers,

performing musicians, college professors, music administrators, and policy leaders. The great diversity of viewpoints expressed in magazines provides music teachers with a wide variety of opinions and suggestions. These are incredibly beneficial to early-career teachers who are looking to find out what other people think about specific topics.

Magazines are more commonly available in print form by subscription. They are often topical and arranged around a certain area of music teaching and learning (e.g., instrumental, secondary general). From the titles of widely-available music magazines listed below, you can see examples of how magazines often cater to a specific audience.

- American Music Teacher
- General Music Today
- In Tune
- The Instrumentalist
- Music Alive!
- Music Educators Journal
- Music Teacher Magazine
- Teaching Music

Engage in Action Research

Equipped with critical reflective tools and a student-centered process for making and evaluating change, early-career music teachers can consider formally researching their own practice. Action research is a systematic process of self-reflection in which teachers seek to better understand, and subsequently improve, their teaching and student learning.[6] It is a more rigorous and public form of self-reflection; teachers engage in action research when they open their action research findings to critical evaluation.[7] Typically, action research projects spiral between observing, planning, acting, and reflecting,[8] in an iterative process of change.

Essentially, action research is a more rigorous version of the self-reflective process outlined in this chapter. We've adapted Creswell's steps for action research:[9]

1. Identify and research a problem
2. Develop a solution
3. Locate necessary resources
4. Implement the plan
5. Collect and analyze data
6. Reflect

Journal entries about your daily, quarterly, and yearly performance provide excellent data for self-analysis. You can use any format that feels most representative of your thoughts, including bulleted lists, prose, blog posts, and tweets. Start by searching for themes in your journal data. Find phrases, thoughts, and ideas that appear frequently; group related ideas together. Each of these groups presents a theme about your practice and can provide insight about assumptions, biases, motivations, and other habits. Student reflections, performance data, progress sheets, and journals offer just a few data points for analysis. This may seem like a lot of information to manage in the first few years of teaching, but you can start working through assumptions and better relate your curriculum to your community by recording and collecting this data early in your career.

Other Resources

Finally, utilize resources that are personally available to you. Other teachers, both within and outside your district, can be your biggest source of support and guidance as you navigate the start of your career. You will find some of the best professional learning occurs outside of your place of employment. Social networking platforms can also be an excellent resource to build professional networks, look for new ideas, or navigate particular challenges.

At some point you may hear a seasoned teacher comment "You're still so full of life and energy, and you still have such a positive outlook on music teaching. I remember when I was a first-year teacher…" They may deliver this message with support and optimism: "Don't give up the good fight!" Anytime you hear this, smile and take it as a compliment. You are capable of helping to advance the profession of music teaching and learning.

Coda

I (Erik) still keep in touch with Addie from time to time, and have guided many other students toward a career in music teaching and learning. I hope that by sharing this story, I was able to help spark some ideas that will also guide you as you continue along your path.

At this point, it might be helpful to provide answers to Addie's questions: How do you motivate students to practice? What do you do to connect with your community? How do you provide enough support for students who are struggling, while still challenging the students who are excelling?

We'll end this chapter with the same wisdom Erik gave Addie: "There are no answers!" Or perhaps Erik should have said "It depends…" As Randall Allsup wrote, we must be content to "muddle" through our profession, constantly doing the best we can for our students.[10]

Chapter 4

Relating Curriculum to Community

Reflect on your school music experiences and remember your favorite teachers. They were probably the people you felt were being "real" with you. They spoke with passion, and you knew their love for music was genuine. They may have been good listeners, and encouraged you to do your best work. As a result, you may have felt you could ask for help without being judged. These teaching practices help to develop student autonomy and motivation. Researchers have found that students are most likely to feel intrinsically motivated to learn when they receive autonomy support from their teachers.[1] As you remember some of your favorite music teachers and how they supported your capacity to learn, realize that you can play a similar role in your community.

Open-mindedness and kindness are traits of someone committed to being a reflective music teacher. Music teachers can develop these traits in their formative years of working to better understand and engage with their communities, and make decisions based on current trends and life experiences of others around them.

This chapter includes ideas and discussion about how reflective music teachers plan and make decisions. Whether making widespread changes or in-the-moment comments, reflective teachers use straightforward language in the context of activities that are relevant, student-centered, and enjoyable.

Facilitating Relatable Activities

Take an interest in students' interests.
Like all relationships, it takes time to build trust between students and teachers, and for students to understand and appreciate your priorities. Take time to learn about genres or cultural forms that are meaningful to your students. Students will see this and appreciate your genuine interest in their futures. This helps to build trust. It can also serve as a point of departure for inquiry-based activities. Learn about the music your students listen to and, when possible, design and facilitate projects around making or re-making this music. For example, if you realize that a student constantly listens to video game music, you might craft a lesson that points out similarities between that music and class repertoire. This valuable use of class time will connect to student interests and increase the value of your class.

Trust your own musicianship.
The more you teach, the more you will learn about young people, about yourself, and about music. *This is a good thing.* As you do, you will likely encounter a lot of different kinds of music, many of which may be new to you. If you assign a songwriting project and a student turns in a song in an unfamiliar style to you, remember you are qualified to give meaningful feedback. Regardless of your musical training — be it classical, contemporary, jazz, etc. — you are still a professional musician in the eyes of your students.

Celebrate connections between your class and life.
Similar to the idea that showing interest in your students' interests builds trust, if students feel that what they learn in your class prepares them for life, their motivation will increase. Show examples of how your curriculum relates to music in the community. Students should feel successful in your classroom, but they should also feel that they are preparing for a life of music. Get excited; be enthusiastic!

Scenarios

The following scenarios illustrate examples of early-career music teachers who design activities related both to instructional objectives and their students' lives. Through use of clear and specific language, these teachers help students make meaningful connections between curriculum and community. In the first scenario, Damon draws upon their extensive musicianship skills to celebrate and expand students' musical interests. In the second scenario, Lana inherits and thoughtfully transforms a high school marching band program while earning the respect of her students and community.

Scenario 4.1: Middle School Choir Teacher

Throughout college, Damon earned a reputation as a knowledgeable and thoughtful music student who could make musical connections between cultural forms and time periods. They could easily relate Bach to bebop, or the middle section of a contemporary choir piece to what was on the radio. Damon frequently found these skills useful during their student teaching placement.

Damon typically gave very specific instructions to their students with appropriate rationale while student teaching. Instead of saying

"Let's sing that phrase better," Damon would direct students to "Sing slightly louder when the notes go up, and get quieter when the notes go down. In this way, we add inflection just like we do when speaking." Unsurprisingly, Damon accepted a job as a full-time middle school choir teacher right out of college because of their music skills and efficient rehearsal technique.

Damon's first class of 35 students was fun and engaging. Perfectly-timed icebreakers, demonstrations, and singing activities went over well, and set the tone for the room as a friendly place with high expectations. In particular, the students enjoyed learning the new pop song Damon wrote over the summer, and especially liked learning how to add harmonies and create a new arrangement of the verses and chorus.

Parents had heard wonderful things about the new choir teacher and were eager to meet Damon at Back-to-School Night. Damon impressed parents with a lighthearted, relaxed demeanor, and obvious passion for music. Not a bad start for a first-year teacher!

Damon's positive and professional relationships with students, parents, and colleagues deepened all year long. Damon typically rehearsed concert music during each class period; students worked together toward a common goal and seemed to enjoy this focused rehearsal time. Students appreciated the diverse repertoire, which typically included classical and contemporary pieces, and a student-arranged selection. Damon commonly drew parallels between seemingly disparate styles of music, such as hip-hop and Renaissance, chiptune and SATB, jazz and baroque. Students also learned about text painting, song form, and the importance of repetition. With this knowledge, students excitedly wrote original compositions and performed them in concert. Having these artifacts also allowed Damon to document student learning and improve instruction.

Reflection

Damon's success was a result of their versatile musicianship and constant consideration of how students could apply class content outside of school. Damon committed to the idea that choir class would prepare students to think inquisitively in addition to performing musically. By consistently facilitating inquiry-based activities, Damon built a culture of deep thought and meaningful music learning in choir class. We would like to highlight several strategies that contributed to Damon's success.

Encourage both convergent and divergent thinking activities.

Peter Webster stressed the importance of creative thinking in music classrooms, suggesting "a combination of convergent and divergent thinking is informed by personal enabling skills and social enabling conditions."[2] Teachers can encourage divergent thinking practices by including music students like to listen to outside of school. Students could analyze "the form" of a piece, and talk about the different "layers" they heard. In this story, Damon used student-selected music to connect similar elements as the music they were learning to perform. By doing this, Damon showed that open-ended activities like composition and improvisation are just as valuable as learning concert music.

Plan new relatable lessons through intentional reflection.

Teachers who document their own practice engage in an incredibly important reflective process. As Annie Mok wrote, "Being a teacher requires a lifelong reflective practice, as well as a drive to pursue professional excellence and advancement in one's career."[3] Damon's visible excitement for divergent thinking and student opinions motivates everyone to learn. Most importantly, Damon's relentless drive to examine and improve their own practice resulted in high levels of student engagement and empowerment.

Scenario 4.2: High School Band Teacher

Before graduating college, Lana made connections with principals and arts supervisors in the state by staying active in the state music education organization, assisting local public school marching bands, and summer camp internship programs. She played in her college's top ensembles and gained recognition for creating new student leadership positions within the music school. When school districts started looking for new teachers during her senior year, Lana's name was at the top of everyone's list and Lana became the first person in her graduating class to be offered a full-time job teaching high school band.

The previous band director retired after a storied, 30-year career, leaving Lana with a program steeped in tradition. Lana felt it was important for the students and community to continue the existing routines, and structured her curriculum around the event calendar left by her predecessor. Rather than trying to alter too much about the curriculum right away, Lana decided to focus on building rapport with her new community by embracing the program's history and traditions.

Lana quickly earned the appreciation of her students, colleagues, and members of the community by teaching the field show announced by her predecessor. She also continued the long tradition of the band singing "The Pride" song at the start of every rehearsal. The annual drill-down competition was still well-attended, and parents wrote letters to the principal praising her obvious knowledge, passion, and commitment to the students. Lana realized her communication style was naturally very effective — her verbal instructions and feedback to students were both direct and positive. Lana also had a knack for recognizing which activities were most relevant to students and which ones were outdated.

Throughout the year, Lana began to identify some traditions that no longer seemed to resonate with her students. For example, some of the military-style commands used in marching band stood in contrast to the current culture of the ensemble. The traditional unifying cheers about sound and pride didn't always lead to a better sound or more pride. But Lana had a plan.

The following year, Lana revamped her rehearsal activities to better connect emerging traditions with her instructional goals. Instead of singing through "The Pride" song, Lana started having the band sing through their show music and noticed an immediate improvement in intonation and articulation. In lieu of a competitive drill-down, which historically celebrated students who could obey marching orders, Lana assigned student leaders to run drill sectionals. Lana began to notice an increased sense of attention to detail among her students, and felt much better about how the band spent rehearsal time. As students' skills improved, their sense of pride deepened. Rehearsals and performances mirrored the personalities of current students, and Lana's reflective praxis continued to evoke meaningful change.

Reflection

Lana quickly earned the trust of her students and their parents by embracing existing traditions and meeting community expectations for the marching band. By also taking a genuine interest in the band program's traditions, Lana quickly built relationships in her school. These foundational relationships proved crucial as she refocused her instruction to relate to current students. When Lana realized some of the traditions of the past didn't support her instructional goals, she gradually incorporated new ones. Lana chose to build on personal relationships to affect positive change in the program which resulted in higher student learning and increased camaraderie.

Building professional connections will eventually benefit your students.

Lana spent her college career taking advantage of opportunities to build music and teaching skills. In addition to completing requirements for her degree, Lana worked with teachers in the state music education organization and local school systems. These experiences provided Lana with invaluable practice that eventually led to her getting a recommendation from an administrator. Importantly, Lana's decision to get involved wasn't based on landing a job, but to get better at teaching music. This distinction is crucial: because Lana's goal was to build her own skills, she earned recognition organically, and students are likely to benefit for years to come.

Positive relationships are a prerequisite for change.

People want the best for their community. While change can be challenging, your administration, learning standards, and students may require it. In this scenario, Lana established rapport with her students and community before changing established traditions. Lana's positive relationships with others, qualifications, and communication skills all contributed to innovation and success. The more you understand community values and expectations, the easier change will be.

Reflective practice keeps students at the center of curricular decisions.

This seems rather obvious! However, in regular lessons it can be easy for teachers to repeat practices that "work" and forget to foreground current student experiences. Lana avoided developing this habit by committing to making decisions that reflected her students' lived experiences. "Student-centered" does not necessarily mean that students request or initiate change, but rather that teachers prioritize learning over tradition. Additionally, Lana did not abruptly decide to make these decisions. They were the result of careful reflection and resulted in increased musical skill and student pride.

Reflective teachers like Lana make sure their decisions maximize student benefits.

Other Suggestions

Brainstorm ideas alongside your students and other stakeholders.

Invite students to participate in lesson planning, music selection, and brainstorm other creative activities. When students' help shape short- and long-term learning goals, teachers have a better understanding of how to make class activities more relatable to students, and can provide more meaningful formative feedback.[4] Involve students in your decision-making process by asking questions like these:

- What do you want to accomplish in choir class this week/month/year?

- What do you think we should spend more/less time working on?

- What would you like to be able to do after taking this class?

> *What other questions might help you discover students' short- and long-term goals so that you can plan relevant lessons?*

Engagement looks different for each student.

Students may display various physical behaviors, especially when thinking critically about new information. While some students will sit up straight, make eye contact, and respond at times you feel are appropriate, others may not. A student gazing around the room may be hearing a musical variation in their head; a student loudly clicking the buttons on their instrument may be "silently" practicing a difficult passage; a student on their phone may be listening to music related to your class or looking up a musical definition. Be mindful of your students' various modes of engagement, especially as you teach new concepts.

Vary the venue, voice, or structure.

Small changes to your class set up can help foster a vibrant and exciting atmosphere. Set up engagements outside of school (e.g., visits to other schools, concert collaborations, performances in community spaces, and trips to concert venues). Invite guests into your teaching space—including staff members from within your building or district, local college professors, and/or military musicians—to provide other valuable musical perspectives. As an added benefit, these guests may help reinforce the concepts you've been teaching all along! Tactful changes in routine will break up monotony and keep your classroom an exciting place to learn. Have students lead parts of your class, teach a lesson on other musical styles, perform for your students, or share favorite recordings and music videos. These small changes will keep your class interesting and lively.

Communicate using positive and specific language.

Students should easily understand your instructions, feedback, questions, and suggestions. Even when encouraging divergent thinking or asking questions with unclear answers, your language should be precise. Keep metaphors consistent and references relevant. Know which colloquialisms to include and which you should avoid. Give some feedback in the form of questions and positive discourse. Most importantly, use specific language. Even when asking open-ended questions, or discussing anything related to creativity, be specific about your intent. Consider how language in these examples provide clarity and rationale:

Ambiguous Language	Specific Language
"When you hear this sound, that means it is time to arrange yourselves by voice part and get to work."	"For the next five minutes, you will work with other people with your same voice part on vowel shapes and the rhythm pattern in the second phrase."
"Make sure you look me in the eyes at all times while I'm teaching."	"Watching the conductor helps ensemble players stay together."
"Stand with amazing posture."	"Relaxed posture and natural breathing are part of healthy technique. Let's practice that now by singing this passage."
"Enjoy the sounds created by these weird chords."	"I like how the tension created by these suspended chords releases at the end of that crescendo. What do you think?"
"Raise your hand every time you hear someone breathe in the wrong place."	"Listen to me sing this phrase for you. Where did I breathe?" [students answer] "Repeat after me."

Summary

When students and community members describe a teacher as "down-to-earth," it is often because the teacher provides rationale for their decisions and encourages questions. Successful teachers facilitate music learning activities that relate to the community. Teachers build trust by engaging students in relatable discussions and activities. Students who feel a connection between their class and their community are likely to experience deeper learning and increased motivation.

- Take an interest in students' interests.
- Trust your own musicianship.
- Celebrate connections between your class and life.
- Encourage both convergent and divergent thinking activities.
- Plan new relatable lessons through intentional reflection.
- Building professional connections benefits students.
- Positive relationships are a prerequisite for change.
- Reflective practice keeps students at the center of curricular decisions.
- Brainstorm ideas alongside your students and other stakeholders.
- Engagement looks different for each student.
- Vary the voice, venue, or class structure.
- Communicate using positive and specific language.

Chapter 5

Creative Musical Activities

Shall we not think twice before we allow the child to consume all his mental power in studying the works of others, and leave no strength or time for his own creative work? Will it not mean more in his development to be able to create one lovely composition than to know accurately the details of all that Chopin ever wrote?
— Satis Coleman[1]

Developing young people's creative abilities is central to meeting [the] purposes of education... As the challenges that face students become more complex, it's essential that schools help them to develop their unique capacities for creative thought and action.
— Ken Robinson and Lou Aronica[2]

At this point in our book, we shift our discussion from reflective thought to reflective practice. Though reflection is certainly something that happens after a lesson or school year, teachers can also use reflection to plan for the future. In this chapter, we build on ideas from previous chapters, and blend ideas about creative musical activities (CMAs) with music technology.

While recent educational discourse highlights the importance of creative musical activities, music teachers have been discussing and facilitating them for the past century. In 1940, Hungarian music educator Ernest Ferand suggested, "the problem of a creative music education seems to be the bridging of the ever-widening gap, first, between active music-making and passive listening, and secondly, between composers and performers."[3] In 1959, the Young Composers Project placed composers in residencies at public schools.[4] The Bennington Institute was founded in the summer of 1962 to foster the development of music teachers' musicianship through composition.[5] In 1966, the Manhattanville Music Curriculum Project aspired to find an alternative path for music education and published a spiral curriculum infused with student-centered creative activities.[6]

In 1994 the Music Educators National Conference (MENC) adopted the National Standards for Music Education, listing "improvisation" and "composition" as critical components of a well-rounded music education. Twenty years later, the National Association for Music Education (NAfME) reimagined these as the National Core Arts Standards, which listed 'Create' as one of four artistic processes.

Music teachers generally believe it is important for students to develop the abilities to improvise, arrange, and compose music,[7] yet activities that result in the generation of original musical material are seldom included in public school curricula.[8] Music teachers perceive numerous obstacles that prevent them from including CMAs. Lack of time, lack of technology and physical space resources, and lack of professional development are commonly cited factors that inhibit the inclusion of such activities in the classroom.[9] Further, lack of training, fear, and feelings of unpreparedness at the undergraduate level may play a role in whether or not beginning teachers choose to include CMAs in the curriculum.[10]

Despite these perceived obstacles, many music teachers choose to consistently and systematically integrate CMAs in music curricula.

These teachers model best teaching practices by providing opportunities and encouragement for students to create original music. Steven Schopp[11] identified four common strategies to teach improvisation and composition: (a) start simple and use limits; (b) allow students to make mistakes; (c) remain flexible to accommodate varied creative learning experiences; and (d) perform student creations in public concerts. Using these strategies, combined with the resources provided at the end of this chapter, teachers may feel empowered to include CMAs in their instructional practice.

Understanding the Creative Process

Research into the creative process exploded in the 1950s and 1960s, and it is nearly impossible to discuss creativity without referencing two pioneers in the field: J.P. Guilford and E. Paul Torrance. Guilford's tests of creative ability and the Torrance Tests of Creative Thinking paved the way for continued research in creativity. Mihalyi Csikszentmihalyi, perhaps best-known for conceiving *Flow* Theory, summarized five recursive (non-linear) stages of the creative process:[12]

1. Preparation – Becoming immersed in a set of problematic issues.
2. Incubation – The brain subconsciously works out possible solutions.
3. Insight – The "Aha!" moment when the best solution becomes clear.
4. Evaluation – A period of reflection to determine the novelty of the insight.
5. Elaboration – A process of exploration and reworking of ideas.

The elaboration phase is where the majority of creative activity occurs, often punctuated by epiphany moments of insight. The creative process is quite similar in structure to the phases in action research, outlined in Chapter 3, in that it spirals between phases. Creativity is often referred to as "big C" Creativity (something eminently novel in society), or "little c" creativity (everyday innovations; something new to the creator). A general understanding of this process may help define creativity in music teaching and learning.

Defining Creativity

What does "creativity" mean to you? Pause here for a moment, and consider how you might define creativity. Now, apply your definition to music education. What does it mean to be creative while learning and making music?

Peter Webster defines creative thinking as "a dynamic mental process that alternates between divergent (imaginative) and convergent (factual) thinking, moving in stages over time."[13] Music teachers often find it easier to encourage convergent thinking in regular instructional activities. Convergent thinking is an important teaching strategy to encourage conceptual transfer and assess student learning. Convergent thinking occurs in situations when a student is expected to come up with the 'correct' answer. For example: "What meter is this song in?", "Is this major or minor tonality?", or "Listen to this song and figure out the harmonic progression." Divergent thinking activities require students to process questions for which there are often multiple, flexible solutions. For example: "What do you think the composer intended in this section?", or "How do you feel when track volumes are automated throughout a piece?" Using your definition, Webster's definition, or some combination of the two, consider the value of these CMAs:

analyzing	composing	moving	playing
arranging	improvising	notating	producing
audiating	listening	performing	singing

Is there musical value in every one of the activities above? Of course! Do you have time to address every one of these activities in your class? Perhaps. Perhaps not. However, by devoting time to a wide variety of CMAs, music teachers can include more musical styles, reach a greater number of students, integrate technology, and align with standards.[14] When planning to include CMAs in instruction, ask yourself the following questions:

- How do CMAs contribute to student learning?
- How do CMAs relate to and reflect the culture of a classroom?
- How do CMAs align with administrative expectations?

These are big questions! Schools, districts, and states may have curriculum maps which can serve as a guideline to help you navigate these questions. Additionally, take the opportunity to discuss new resources, school traditions, and innovative ideas with experienced teachers—these conversations often spark rich dialogue among your colleagues. Integrating CMAs in your curriculum is a great way to address current educational buzzwords: learner agency, 21st century skills, learner agency, autonomy, and collaboration. The National Association for Music Education (NAfME.org) provides free access to many advocacy resources, and the National Coalition for Core Arts Standards (NationalArtsStandards.org) details anchor standards and sample assessments relating to CMAs.

Generative Musical Activities

While there are an infinite number of musical activities that may be considered creative we now turn our attention to those that are inherently generative. According to Estelle Jorgensen, "In music education, the terms composing, arranging, and improvising are generally linked under the umbrella of 'creative' musical activities."[15] We will use the following definitions:

- Composing – creating and preserving original, meaningful musical ideas with the opportunity to reflect and revise.

- Arranging – creating original, meaningful versions of pre-existing musical ideas and works.

- Improvising – creating original, meaningful musical ideas in the moment of performance.

Whether or not you feel prepared to teach these activities, your music training experience gives you the theory and aural skills knowledge to include CMAs with your students. Trust yourself, and use your musical strengths to lead students through these activities. You are prepared and qualified to engage students in these activities, even if you do not personally identify as a composer, producer, or improvisor. This provides an excellent opportunity for you to learn alongside your students, and model hard work and perseverance.

You will have more success teaching students to improvise, arrange, and compose when they see you practicing these activities yourself. The more opportunities you and your students have to learn and create music together, the more collaborative and enjoyable the learning process becomes. Process and product are not mutually exclusive. The *process* of generating original music can also be the *product*; it is not so much the quality of the finished product that matters, as the quality of the creative musical experience.

Ideas about Music Technology

There are countless ways to include composing, arranging, and improvising into existing teaching situations, and can involve multiple technologies. Arguably, every musical instrument beyond the human voice could be considered a "technology." While we often consider music technology to include such items as tablets, laptops, or other tools to digitally create and manipulate music, it also encompasses metronomes, tuners, microphones, audio interfaces… and even music notation! Everything from optical cables to acoustically designed sound-absorbing acoustic panels to the electric piano was initially a new technology developed to improve the musical experience. Technology in music teaching and learning situations is not a new idea — we've been using it for as long as we've been teaching music!

With such a potentially broad understanding of technology, we employ "music technology" to refer to any object that may be utilized to enable musical exploration and discovery that leads to increased musical comprehension. Importantly, this definition requires that the technology functions to increase musical comprehension. To the extent that technology replaces human-initiated decisions, it ceases to contribute to increased musical comprehension, and could hinder the creative musical process. For example, students who are required to use a music notation program may spend less time in the elaboration phase of creativity, as the notation may concretize emerging musical ideas.[16] We join Jennifer Slack and J. Macgreggor Wise in cautioning against the mindset that more technology is always better.[17] Music technologies are tools that demand methodical approaches centered around exploration, discovery, and understanding. Teachers must consider how technologies enable student-centered musical expression, and contribute to curricular goals and lesson objectives.

Technology has tremendous potential to meet the needs of students marginalized in traditional music settings. It can also (a) be a powerful tool to help develop creative musicianship, (b) be used as a means to realize musical ideas, or (c) exist interdependently with the creative musical process. Our goal for this portion of the chapter is to focus on several considerations of technology to mediate the creative process. The following scenario describes a conversation among four music teachers regarding technology integration and popular music.

Scenario 5.1: "Do your students ever ask you how to...?"

Four close friends Howard, Rose, Elyse, and Mike carpooled to the annual state music education conference. After graduating college two years earlier, they all started work teaching music in the same city. On the long drive, they caught up about work and life. They told jokes, listened to music on the radio, and played classic car games. Eventually, the conversation turned toward the conference schedule. They noticed sessions related to each of their jobs (band, choir, orchestra), and sessions about general music, teacher education, and a session called "Music Technology That Works for You." Rose asked, "So, how do you guys use technology in your classes? Do any of your schools even have tablets? Mine only has a few." The consensus in the car was that technology was just sort of around, but that it wasn't really part of their curriculum. When the conversation died down, the only sound in the car was the music on the radio.

When the next hip-hop song came on, Elyse asked, "Do your students ever ask you how to make music like this?"

Howard and Mike shook their heads. Rose responded, "Not really."

Elyse continued, "This is how music is in the world. Why is it not like this in the classroom?"

Howard and Mike shrugged. After a few seconds, Rose looked out the window and said, "I feel like you just have to have a lot of technology to make this music."

"Yeah, but it can't be that hard to do," Elyse replied. "I know some of my kids make beats and put them on social media. I just wonder if it's even possible to do that in a music class."

Elyse and Rose talked for a few minutes about how technology, which they agreed was ubiquitous, helps musicians be more creative. Elyse mused, "In a perfect world, I think technology and music could be part of the classroom, but we really don't have time to teach other things. And we don't want to sacrifice the quality of the music in our class."

Howard interjected, "No. Because when I think about how I learned music and how kids learn best… music technology can assist me in developing my musicianship. Electronic devices—tuners, recording gear, synthesizers—these are all tools that help a person develop a sense of pitch, steady time, amplify voices, or add sounds to a performance. There are other uses, too."

Elyse pressed, "But what makes electronic devices special? Why aren't they considered instruments themselves? I mean, aren't cellos and flutes just devices without electricity?"

The other three paused to contemplate Elyse's question. Mike broke the silence. "But, once I develop my musicianship, I can apply it in some way to music technology if I choose to. For example, if I am a good musician first, I could use my laptop to record a pop song I write, or record my jazz soloing. But, fundamental musicianship is crucial to have before diving into techn…"

Elyse cut Mike off, "But if your laptop *is* your instrument, can't this help you develop your musicianship, just like your saxophone does?"

"But the laptop does all the work for you," Mike retorted. "You don't have to think to use a laptop. You can just drag-and-drop loops and press play."

"You also don't have to think to press piano keys. The piano makes sound for you," Elyse replied, smiling.

"Yea but if you use a laptop, *you're not the one making the music, the laptop is!*"

Rose, who had been listening, said softly, "Maybe you need to use the laptop better."

"What?" the other three said in unison.

"Well, any of these 'technologies' can be used, taught, and learned badly. Or they can be used well. I don't know if anyone is right here, but I think it's all in how you approach using it."

Rose continued, "Music learning and making and music technology are symbiotic and always have been. 'Music technology' is a rebranding of 'music tools,' which have been made and used by humans since the dawn of time. Everything from a laptop to a trumpet to a pencil has at one time been considered technology. To me, these tools all have the same potential to contribute to a person's musical life. It all depends on how they—the tools—are valued by the person using them. This is the only thing that truly matters."

"Boom!" Elyse yelled.

Mike, who was unconvinced, said, "But I don't think that's very practical. Like, how does this apply to me and my kids? Kids just want to sound good. It's our job to make them sound good."

"Yeah, I think kids just want to be part of something, and they need to learn to be part of something bigger than themselves," Howard said while turning down the radio volume.

"But can't technology help kids sound good in their own way?" Rose replied. "We would just need to rethink our class goals."

Elyse turned up the radio again while saying, "Well to make this kind of music, the kind of music all around us, we need some technology. Let's go to that tech session and see if we can find a way to do this in our classes."

Reflection

Howard, Mike, and Rose all had different ideas about how to define music technology, and in music teaching and learning. Elyse, who started the conversation, recognized a difference between the music playing on the radio and classroom music. She questioned this discrepancy, and found her friends all had different perspectives. Consider how Howard, Mike, and Rose viewed music technology as it relates to music learning and making.

Howard: Music Technology → Music Learning and Making

Howard defined music technology as strictly electronic devices that assist, not define, someone's musical development. Tuners, recording systems, and synthesizers are examples of tools that can help develop someone's sense of pitch, steady pulse, aural skills, and awareness of audio manipulation techniques to augment live or recorded performances.

Mike: Music Learning and Making → Music Technology

Mike also defined music technology as electronic devices that can supplement music learning. Tools like digital audio workstations (DAWs), microphones, and audio interfaces are technologies that help musicians create products, but only after musical ideas already exist in their heads. While technologies can permanatize ideas, foundational learning happens on classroom instruments without electricity.

Rose: Music Learning and Making ↔ Music Technology

More than Mike or Howard, Rose believed a methodical approach to using any tool was more important than the tool itself, and could lead to a variety of outcomes. Music technologies have learning and creative implications. Students can learn and make music through simultaneous (a) exploration of technology and (b) exploration using technology. We provide examples of what this might look like in a classroom at the end of this chapter (see "Designing Musical Projects").

Elyse: "I just wonder if it's even possible to do that in a music class."

When Elyse questioned the feasibility of making radio-style music in her classroom, she began to unpack inherent assumptions that guided her curriculum. Even by asking reflective questions like the one above, Elyse questioned "the way it's always been done" and how to better relate her class to her community. While there are no perfect answers to Elyse's question, we submit that early-career reflection is paramount to progress.

> *Have a discussion with a colleague about these and other views related to "music making and learning" and "music technology." Here are a few questions to guide your conversation:*
>
> 1. Which views do you associate with some of your former teachers?
> 2. Which views are most practical in different situations (i.e., performance, recruiting, enrollment, meeting learning standards, etc.)?
> 3. Which views are most likely to include or exclude students with special needs and diverse backgrounds and interests?

Music Technology ↔ Creative Musical Activities

Creative musical activities and technology constantly interact in classrooms and communities. When making curricular decisions as an early-career music teacher, consider the idea that music teaching and learning involves various technologies that influence instruction. These technologies range from musical instruments, to various forms of music notation, to electronic and print publications, and to digital music tools. We encourage you to conceptualize music technology both as a set of tools that facilitate music teaching and learning, and as a freestanding curriculum with its own standards, methods, and assessments.

The National Core Arts Standards include a Music Technology Strand that encourages students to create; perform, present, and produce; respond; and connect.[18] When students discover how to produce and share original music, they realize their creative and lifelong potential for music making. Technologies—whether laptops, smartphones, or MIDI controllers—can function as primary access points for someone's musical development and expression. Creative experiences with technologies can occur in any music class; they already occur outside music class.

Similar to leading students through potentially unfamiliar CMAs, use your musical strengths and training (i.e., knowledge of repertoire and aural skills) to experiment with technologies. There is no need to feel like an expert before starting. In fact, you will have more success teaching students to explore and make music with technology when they see you learning at the same time.

Students who express interest in music technology as primary or assistive tools may be willing to share their knowledge with you and other students. By facilitating student-led lessons, not only will you increase your technological literacy, but you will increase learner agency and autonomy, and empower other students to pursue their own musical interests outside of your class.

Staying Open to Different Musics

There is a good chance you will have different musical preferences from your students, though there will undoubtedly be some overlap.

Differences in age, previous musical experiences, extent of formal study, and personal preference all contribute to the development of unique musical tastes and practices. Regardless of these differences, students are going to like the music they like — it may be the reason they enrolled in a music class in the first place. You can help your students develop their musical praxis while concurrently teaching them to better understand it.

The beauty of music is in its diversity: virtually everybody can discover music they enjoy listening to and making! As technology continues to expand, we have unprecedented access to music from around the world and the ability to create music that we enjoy. Outside of Western classical music (with which you may be most familiar), melody and harmony are often subordinate to lyrics and poetry. Some popular musics rarely change chords, and many do not use any of the instruments commonly found in music teaching and learning institutions. David Elliott reminds us that "MUSIC, as a diverse human practice, is central to the constitution of cultural and individual identities."[19] Diverse musical forms, styles, timbres, and communities intersect throughout the world, and should be represented in our classrooms.

While planning lessons, relate your instruction to musics you personally enjoy, as well as to those that may have inspired your students to study music. Invite students to share their favorite music. Ask them questions about the music they enjoy: "Tell me what you like about this music. What do you hear? How is it made?" Use this as an opportunity to develop deeper listening skills and introduce new vocabulary (e.g., verse, chorus, hook, sample, autotune, and reverb) into your discussions.

In the end, you may discover that you do not like your students' favorite music, and they may or may not learn to like yours. However, you will likely find they are more willing to learn to appreciate a wide variety of music when you are willing to learn about the music that is important and meaningful to them. It is through greater understanding that we will develop the capacity for greater appreciation.

Making Music to Share Music

While you and your students improvise, arrange, and compose together, think about how to share these products, with friends, parents, and the community. The first, easiest opportunity to share student creations may just be an in-class performance; you can have a show and tell for students who are willing to share. This is also a great opportunity to develop listening and analytical skills while nurturing a climate of collaboration.

When your students have developed a portfolio of musical creations, you could expand this in-class performance by inviting other teachers, classes, administrators, or board of education members to join you. You might feature student compositions on a concert night, or arrange a band, orchestra, or chorus piece to incorporate an improvisatory section. Interested students may even produce a musical, rewrite your school's alma mater, or publish a book of in-class compositions. Over time, your traditional concerts may start to include more and more student-generated content. Time spent teaching notes and rhythms may be reallocated to time for CMAs. Researchers have shown these activities do not diminish performance ability, but instead enhance it.[20]

> **Additional Tips**
> - Start small. Find one activity you are interested in, and try it. If it doesn't go well, choose another one or try again.
> - Solicit student ideas. They may come up with a creative musical activity you hadn't considered.
> - Provide musical options, and allow students to make choices. Students are more likely to continue an activity they have chosen themselves.
> - Avoid the urge to grade everything. Nothing kills creativity like the pressure of being judged and evaluated.
> - Celebrate student successes. Genuine praise will boost confidence and willingness to continue the activity.

Resources

There are myriad resources available to teachers who are looking for ideas to incorporate more CMAs. The following lists are organized by the following categories: Lesson Plans, Creative Thinking, and Music Education Texts. These lists are certainly not all-inclusive, but should provide a starting point for future inquiry. We encourage you to add additional resources that are relatable and important to your community of learners.

Lesson Plans

Developing Musicianship Through Improvisation, by Christopher Azzara & Richard Grunow (GIA Publications)

Engaging Musical Practices, by Suzanne Burton & Alden Snell (Rowman & Littlefield)

Music Outside the Lines: Ideas for Composing in K-12 Music Classrooms, by Maud Hickey (Oxford)

Musicianship: Composing in Band and Orchestra, by Clint Randles and David Stringham (GIA Publications)

Musicianship: Composing in Choir, by Jody Kerchner and Katherine Strand (GIA Publications)

Musicianship: Improvising in Band and Orchestra, by David Stringham and Christian Bernhard (GIA Publications)

Shaping Sound Musicians, by Patricia O'Toole (GIA Publications)

Creative Thinking

Creative Schools, by Ken Robinson and Lou Aronica (Penguin)

Creative Quest, by Questlove (HarperCollins)

Creativity, by Mihaly Csikszentmihalyi (HarperCollins)

Free Play, by Stephen Nachmanovitch (Tarcher-Penguin)

The Mind's Ear, by Bruce Adolphe (Oxford)

Academic/Educational Texts

The Cambridge Handbook of Creativity, by James Kaufman and Robert Sternberg (Cambridge)

Composing Our Future, by Michelle Kaschub and Janice Smith (Oxford)

The Improvising Mind, by Aaron Berkowitz (Oxford)

Musical Creativity: Insights from Music Education Research, by Oscar Odena (Routledge)

Ready, Set, Improvise!: The Nuts and Bolts of Music Improvisation, by Suzanne Burton & Alden Snell (Oxford)

Teaching Music Through Composition: A Curriculum Using Technology, by Barbara Freedman (Oxford)

Chapter 6

Synthesizing Ideas

The ideas we presented in this book emerged from constant reflection and our own personal desires to continue to improve as music teachers and learners. Part of our growth has come through consumption of research, which we have used to ground our process of reflection. Depending on where you are in your (pre-)teaching career, some ideas are likely to resonate more strongly with you. New teachers, and even experienced teachers working in a brand new setting, may initially focus on the general and music-specific advice we offered in Chapter 1. As you gain experience, you will discover which teaching techniques and tools work best for you. As you develop comfortable teaching routines, you will find the space and time to thoughtfully consider your values and reflect on the assumptions that underlie your instructional decisions. You may discover assumptions beyond those outlined in Chapter 2 that influence your curriculum, teaching style, and instructional decisions.

Excellent teachers constantly strive to better relate their curriculum to their students, and relentlessly seek ways to improve the quality of their instruction. There is no point at which you should feel you "figured it all out." Over time, the self-reflective habits we described in Chapter 3 will become a normal function of your musical praxis. We encourage you to be patient as you work through successes and challenges. Remember: change takes time and tenacity. We hope that this collection of ideas serves as a point of departure as you continue to grow as a music teacher and learner, but recognize that there is no *right way* to teach.

As you reflect on your own teaching practices and ideas, you will inevitably find ways to institute meaningful change. As we stressed in Chapter 4, keep students at the center of your curricular decisions. Your lesson plans should evolve to represent the ideas you find most valuable and relatable to your students. The greatest gift you can give your students is the ability to continue learning and making music for the rest of their lives. Help them find their musical voices. Teach them to better understand the music they love so that they can create their own. Using ideas from Chapter 5, find creative ways to utilize technology as you teach students to improvise, arrange, and compose.

Three Example Projects

To help you get started, we have included example projects for you to adapt to your setting based on your available technology, curricular goals, and musical objectives. These projects share a similar focus: to encourage students to think deeply while developing musical understanding. You can tailor each project to a whole classroom or a small group of students, alter assignments based on student interest and ability, and augment or diminish the scope of a project. At the end of each project, we encourage you to reflect using the Post-Project Reflection Questions at the end of the chapter.

Example Project #1: Student Compositions Inspired by Class Repertoire

Description: Students and teachers will demonstrate understanding of tonality (tonic-dominant relationships in major) and meter (triple meter) by creating (improvising, composing, or arranging) parts that accompany class repertoire, or original music. Students will also build understanding of technique (instrumental, vocal, or production).

Possible Tools: instrument, free/paid DAW, notation software, staff paper

The teacher will	while the student
① point out a section of music you're working on in class that has obvious musical elements (harmony, meter, compositional technique),	learns to identify what the teacher points out in your concert music. It might be something about chords, rhyths, or structure.
② have students sing and play what you're talking about. This might require students to learn a new part by ear. Reinforce proper technique. Introduce new terms to help students identify this element in the future,	realizes you are taking a break from working on the whole piece. They may feel surprised by the change of pace. With many reps, they get more comfortable singing and can see the teacher's excitement.
③ ask students to make something musical that contains this element and provide examples which might include producing a new beat, writing a countermelody, transcribing a different part, etc. Continue introducing new terms and techniques as they arise,	may feel comfortable enough to try something but doesn't know how to start until seeing examples. They may need more review, examples, and support. They may think, "Yes! I've always wanted to know how to know how to do this!"
④ show enthusiasm and support while students try, make mistakes and succeed,	realizes their new knowledge of music and how it relates to their own life and performance.

Example Project #2: Making Musical Choices with Multi-Track Automation

Description: Students and teachers will explore musical elements (dynamics, tempo, balance, gain structure, signal flow, and audio effects) by recording and mixing multiple tracks of original or arranged music. Students will work together on all parts of this project.

Possible Tools: paid/free DAW, USB mic or XLR mic + interface, MIDI controller

	The teacher will	while the student
1	provide students with appropriate gear. This may or may not include their school instrument. Try it with and without!	tries to plug in, turn on, play around. There's no need to wait for the teacher if they want to get started!
2	use a USB mic, MIDI controller, or audio interface to make sure each student has a good signal flow (i.e., the computer should be getting sound from your device),	finds system settings or preferences in both the audio program and computer. If they can't hear anything, make sure I/O (input/output) settings match what gear they are using.
3	suggest setting a BPM/tempo first,	learns that "BPM" = tempo.
4	demo the recording process, including how to record, stop, go back, duplicate tracks, assign software instruments, and basic cut/paste,	sees that (a) it's easy to get started, (b) their teacher is enjoying it, (c) they can work with their friends, and (d) their creativity is going to count in this project.
5	give students a time allotment and let them work in small groups! After they are up and running, there is no need to hover,	feels a sense of autonomy and rigor as they start to work with their friends without the teacher, and laugh while exploring and recording new sounds.
6	demonstrate automation, including how to change volume and tempo, and add effects. Connect these terms and processes to others studied in class,	begins mixing multiple tracks. They will get very picky about making sure everything lines up, and connects concepts like balance, blend, and time, to their own product.
7	have students export their work as an audio file, and share,	enjoys the culminating experience. Students discover, maybe for the first time, that they have a unique musical voice.

Synthesizing Ideas 83

Example Project #3: New Arrangements & Community Engagement

Description: Students and teachers will demonstrate understanding of musical elements (form, melody, harmony, and timbre) by arranging a piece of familiar music. This begins by arranging a tune as a class without notation, then sharing their work with others. They will engage members of the community through virtual and in-person music platforms.

Possible Tools: free web-based DAW, web-based notation programs, internet access

The teacher will	while the student
(1) creatively demonstrate playing a familiar melody in a different style (e.g., pop song melody in the style of a concert piece, folk tune in swing style),	tries to memorize the tune, and find the starting note. They recognize the tune, but may have never been asked to play it by ear. They see the teacher get excited by this.
(2) teach the melody to students by ear. Some will get it right away, others will need help. Keep demonstrating, keep helping,	succeeds or searches for the right notes. By this time, the tune is ingrained in their head, so they know what sounds right and wrong.
(3) demonstrate a compatible part you made on a DAW, app, or with another student. Ask your students for input and ideas. Provide several more examples.	realizes they can use their devices, other instruments, and friends to complete this assignment. They hear everyone else making mistakes, too. Anxiety lessens, and fun beings.
(4) teach students how to make their own parts (using notation software, an app, DAW, other instrument, etc.). Be patient and encouraging. This is a great time to learn other instruments,	looks forward to this part of class each day when they can share what they made at home on their phone or learned by watching YouTube videos. The teacher always gives feedback.
(5) build an arrangement with your students by discussing form (e.g., intro, melody, solos, pre-chorus, hit, chorus). Show the same zeal for this as you do other tasks,	gets ideas for their own arrangement. They enjoy working on this project with the whole class, but since starting this kind of thing, they have a lot of ideas for their own arrangements.
(6) invite members of the community, parents, and staff to go through this process with you and your students. Expand this activity into a concert, open jam session, or virtual meeting. Stress that any musician is welcome,	is excited because their class' arrangement is getting performed. Even better, some of the other teachers and siblings are joining in!

> **Post-Project Self-Reflection Questions**
> After each project session, ask yourself these questions:
>
> - What did students appear to like/dislike?
> - How do you think the project connected to students' musical futures?
> - How did students react to various types of feedback (written list, verbal, public, private)?
> - What assumptions can you challenge in this lesson (see Chapter 2)?
> - Based on your answers to these questions, what should you continue or change about your practice?

Feedback

Reflective and educated teachers like you are more than qualified to learn and give feedback on any type of music. Your students may have already explored and experimented with some form of music technology, and will not rely exclusively on you for instruction. The internet is packed with free tutorials on everything from performance to recording and mixing techniques. Here's what students can't get on the internet: instant feedback from you. You are not replaceable, and you may be the only professional musician your student has access to. So, remember to trust your musicianship, especially when a student shows interest in musical forms that are less familiar to you.

Whenever you give feedback, keep it short, related, and open-ended. Use specific language (see Chapter 4) that leaves room for students to grow. Here are two templates that help organize specific feedback. The first is designed for a teacher to fill out in their own words. The second is a bank of comments that students might have created. Have your students make their own.

music technology

MULTI-TRACK FEEDBACK

student:　　　　　　　date:　　　　　　　project:

MEASURE/TIME	PART/TRACK	FEEDBACK

Check out these recordings/artists:

music technology

COMMON COMMENTS
student-generated form and comments

student: date: project:

circle all that apply

VOCALS
autotune vocals at ____   reduce clipping at ____   reduce reverb ____
decompress ____   add reverb ____   add compression at ____
balance volume at ____   control dynamics at ____   reduce attack at ____
apply noise gate at ____   boost vocals at ____   reduce sibilance at ____
DRUMS
add EQ to sample drums   add reverb to snare   boost the low-ends
add high-end punch   compress kick drums   use HPF   use LPF on ____
apply soft clipper to 808   pitch 808/kicks to key of the melody
sidechain bass to your kick
SYNTH / KEYS / GUITARS
vary to match other instrumentation   keep notes are on the beat/quantise
add melodic variation to your motifs
make sure all notes are in the same key as your melodies
keep melodic instruments in appropriate ranges (not too high/low)
MIX
add plugins to your tracks (compression, reverb, etc.)
make sure no track clips in your whole session
keep 1/2 track(s) in balance with the rest of the mix at ____
keep tracks varied but not too unrelated at ____
make sure drums are under the melody, usually vocals
use EQ sparingly on separate tracks
MASTER
add soft clipper to master track   add more compression to master track
apply adaptive limiter   add harmonic booster/exciter

other comments:

Notes

Chapter 1

[1] Allsup & Benedict, 2008, p. 158. Allsup and Benedict discussed the problems of tradition, method, legitimacy, social history, change, and pedagogy.

[2] See Robinson, 2015.

[3] Connelly & Clandinin, 1988, p. 124.

[4] Robert Duke (2005) identified specific components of what musicians do, and encouraged music teachers to define goals in terms of specific musical behaviors. When teachers assign grades, they must be able to justify those grades through explicit behaviors.

[5] Sallaz, 2010, p. 323.

[6] Ryan & Deci, 2017, p. 349. Ryan & Deci cite case studies that support the idea that providing *rationale* promotes an autonomy-supportive environment in parenting, counseling, and education.

[7] Mantie & Talbot, 2015, pp. 129–130.

[8] Change is difficult! Several researchers have discussed obstacles preventing teachers from changing instructional practice. Gatt (2009) reported lack of "top-down" support for innovative teaching practices prohibited many teachers from participating in PD opportunities. "Bottom-up" approaches often fail due to lack of organizational support. Kent (2019) reported the biggest challenge to teachers continuing to implement innovative practices was pressure from

within the building to revert to a more traditional teaching pedagogy. Antinluoma et al. (2018) reported lack of scheduled collaborative time was the biggest challenge facing teachers.

9. In this book, Carol Dweck (2006) describes how maintaining a "growth mindset" (versus "fixed mindset") helps people operate with less tension and more humility. Teachers who have a grown mindset may be more adept at reflecting on and revising their practice.

Chapter 2

1. Allsup & Benedict, 2008, p. 157.
2. Lamaison & Bourdieu, 1986, p. 113.
3. Colleen Conway (2005) wrote a literature review of the experiences of first-year music teachers, and has authored numerous other studies of early-career music teachers.
4. See Connelly and Clandinin (1988) pp. 153–155 for further discussion on the *null* and *hidden curriculum*. Quote from p. 155.
5. Boonshaft, 2006, p. 165. This idea comes from his chapter on Excellence, pp. 163–167. Boonshaft also has several other inspirational books: Teaching Music with Passion, and Teaching Music with Passion, Purpose, and Promise.
6. The Institute for Composer Diversity, founded and directed by Dr. Rob Deemer, was recently formed to "advance an environment in which historically underrepresented groups are fully represented and supported." This website provides a free resource to music teachers looking to diversify their performance repertoire, and includes an Orchestra Season Analysis from which this data was sourced.
7. Grunow, Gordon, & Azzara, 1999, p. 26. Private lessons certainly benefit students who have developed advanced audiation skills, and provide students with individualized attention. Many students learn best, especially at beginning stages, from other students.
8. National Coalition for Core Arts Standards, 2016.
9. For more information about infant musical abilities, we suggest exploring music cognition studies. Sandra Trehub and Laurel Trainor are two of the biggest names in infant music research. Some notable studies: Hannon and Trehub (2005); Mampe et al. (2009); Nakata and Trehub (2004); Trainor et al. (2002).

10 Nachmanovitch, 1990, pp. 135–136. In the chapter on "The Judging Spectre" (pp. 133–139), Nachmanovitch focuses on one of the Five Fears of Buddhism: fear of speaking before an assembly. This fear is also manifest in fear of speaking up, stage fright, and writers block.

11 Gouzouasis and Ryu, 2015, p. 406. This autoethnographic narrative describes the experience teaching a 4-year old piano student in a private studio. The authors highlighted the importance of social growth and personal connection, and encourage teachers to discover the stories that matter most to students so that they may nurture imagination and curiosity.

12 Siebert, 2008, p. 104. Siebert explored reasons music teachers remain in the field through a self-determination theoretical framework. In addition to supplies, a viable curriculum, an autonomy-supportive environment, and appropriate professional development, Siebert found "Music colleagues are essential to career music educators, and they help to make each others' work meaningful and uplifting" (p. vii).

13 Schuster & Finkelstein, 2008, p. 324. Though this assertion is based on survey data from 2003, the authors suggest "contingent full-time and part-time staffing are now the chief modes of institutional operation" (p. 324) and suggest the percentage of contingent faculty continues to rise.

14 See Robinson, 2015.

Chapter 3

1 See Teach Tomorrow (2020) and American School Counselor Education (2020) for tables of professional development requirements by state.

2 https://scholar.google.com/intl/en/scholar/about.html

3 https://ies.ed.gov/ncee/projects/eric.asp

4 https://about.jstor.org/

5 https://www.proquest.com/about/

6 Creswell, 2005, p. 550.

7 McNiff & Whitehead, 2005.

8 Norton, 2018.

9 Creswell, 2005, pp. 562–565.

[10] Allsup, 2016, p. 141. In Remixing the Classroom, Allsup advanced an open philosophy of music education that moves away from a teacher-directed, practice-specific, bounded system and toward a learner-centered, human- and place-specific, demographic system. Allsup encouraged music teachers to "wonder and wander" through the profession. In order to move toward more openness, music teachers—and music teacher educators—must be willing to wade through and embrace the unknown.

Chapter 4

[1] Deci and Ryan, 1985. In this comprehensive review of empirical research, Deci and Ryan outline the framework of Self-Determination Theory. The authors provide a useful table of teacher behaviors that compares autonomy-supportive and controlling behaviors (p. 368).

[2] Webster, 2016, p. 28. In this article, Webster reflected on the previous 25 years of creative thinking in music education. This article was a follow-up to a previous article in which he described the creative music thinking process (Webster, 1990).

[3] Mok, 2016, p. 67. Although Mok conducted this study with pre-service music teachers, she suggested that reflective practices among the participants are also valuable to practicing music teachers.

[4] David Nicol and Debra Macfarlane-Dick (2006) wrote an essay on formative assessment and self-regulated learning that offers context for "good feedback practice."

Chapter 5

[1] Coleman, 1922, p. 179. Coleman raised the concern of standardization in musical training in this early text designed to plan musical training around the 'natural' evolution of music.

[2] Robinson & Aronica, 2015, p. 136. Ken Robinson is most famously known for his TED Talk "Do Schools Kill Creativity?", the most watched talk in the history of TED (p. xvi).

[3] Ferand, 1940, p. 25.

[4] Mark et al., 1999.

[5] Moon, 2006.

6 Thomas, 1970.

7 Fairfield, 2010; Koops, 2009; Snell, 2013.

8 Blockland, 2014; Fairfield, 2010; Schopp, 2006; Strand, 2006; Zitek, 2008.

9 Byo, 1999; Fairfield, 2010; Menard, 2015; Schopp, 2006; Snell, 2013; Strand, 2006.

10 Adderley, 1996; Bernhard & Stringham, 2016; Piazza & Talbot, in press; Snell, 2013.

11 Schopp, 2006.

12 Csikszentmihalyi, 2015, pp. 79–80.

13 Webster, 1990, p. 28.

14 Webster, 2016, p. 27.

15 Jorgensen, 2008, p. 166.

16 Several researchers have indicated notation may inhibit compositional creativity. Alexander Koops (2009) recognized the importance of music notation, but identified it as a separate skill that may hinder the composition process. Michael Hopkins (2015) found that students spent more time on-task playing their instruments, rather than talking about the music, in the absence of notation. In a later study, Hopkins (2019) found "the presence of a notation template in the composing sessions clearly influenced the approach taken by participants" (p. 83). He suggested students might have experimented with more trial run-throughs if he had withheld a notation template until later in the research design.

17 Slack & Wise, 2015, p. 13. This introduction to culture and technology explores cultural assumptions through concepts of articulation and assemblage. Though not specifically focused on music, the ideas in this book are tangentially related to our experiences of music as mediated by technology.

18 National Coalition for Core Arts Standards, 2015.

19 Elliott, 1995, p. 185.

20 See Azzara, 1992; Dodson, 1980; Stoltzfus, 2005; Whitman, 2001. Each of these authors report that including regular improvisation or composition activities in place of some traditional instruction led to increased performance on select variables.

References

Adderley, Cecil Leopole, III. (1996). *Music teacher preparation in South Carolina colleges and universities relative to the national standards: Goals 2000*. (Publication No. 9711655) [Doctoral dissertation, University of South Carolina]. ProQuest Dissertations Publishing.

Allsup, Randall Everett. (2016). *Remixing the classroom: Toward an open philosophy of music education*. Indiana University Press.

Allsup, Randall Everett, & Benedict, Cathy. (2008). The problems of band: An inquiry into the future of instrumental music education. *Philosophy of Music Education Review, 16*(2), 156–173. https://doi.org/10.2979/PME.2008.16.2.156

American School Counselor Education. (2020). *Continuing Education Requirements*. https://www.schoolcounselor.org/school-counselors-members/careers-roles/continuing-education-requirements

Antinluoma, Markku, Ilomäki, Liisa, Lahti-Nuuttila, Pekka, & Toom, Auli. (2018). Schools as professional learning communities. *Journal of Education and Learning, 7*(5), 76–91. https://doi.org/10.5539/jel.v7n5p76

Azzara, Christopher D. (1992). *The effect of audiation-based improvisation techniques on the music achievement of elementary instrumental music students*. (Publication No. 9223853) [Doctoral dissertation, University of Rochester]. ProQuest Dissertations Publishing.

Bernhard, H. Christian, & Stringham, David A. (2016). A national survey of music education majors' confidence in teaching improvisation. *International Journal of Music Education, 34*(4), 383-390. https://doi.org/10.1177/0255761415619069

Blockland, Cheryl A. (2014). *Teaching improvisation: A survey of secondary string music teachers in Maryland and Virginia*. (Publication No. 3722177) [Doctoral dissertation, Shenandoah University]. ProQuest Dissertations Publishing.

Boonshaft, Peter Loel. (2006). *Teaching music with purpose: Conducting, rehearsing and inspiring*. Meredith Music Publications.

Byo, Susan J. (1999). Classrooms teachers' and music specialists' perceived ability to implement the national standards for music education. *Journal of Research in Music Education, 47*(2), 111-123. https://doi.org/10.2307/3345717

Coleman, Satis N. (1922). *Creative music for children, a plan of training based on the natural evolution of music, including the making and playing of instruments, dancing – singing – poetry*. G. P. Putnam's Sons.

Connelly, F. Michael, & Clandinin, D. Jean. (1988). *Teachers as curriculum planners: Narratives of experience*. Teachers College Press.

Conway, Colleen. (2015). The experiences of first-year music teachers: A literature review. *Update: Applications of Research in Music Education, 33*(2), 65-72. https://doi.org/10.1177/8755123314547911

Creswell, John E. (2005). *Educational research: Planning, conducting, and evaluating quantitative and qualitative research* (2nd. ed.). Pearson Education, Inc.

Deci, Edward L., & Ryan, Richard M. (2002). *Handbook of self-determination research*. University of Rochester Press.

Dodson, Thomas A. (1980). The effects of a creative-comprehensive approach and a performance approach on acquisition of music fundamentals by college students. *Journal of Research in Music Education, 28*(2), 103-110. https://doi.org/10.1177/002242948002800203

Duke, Robert A. (2011). *Intelligent music teaching: Essays on the core principles of effective instruction*. Learning and Behavior Resources.

Dweck, Carol S. (2006). *Mindset: The new psychology of success*. Ballantine Books.

Elliott, David J. (1995). *Music matters: A new philosophy of music education*. Oxford University Press.

Fairfield, Sarah Mae. (2010). *Creative thinking in elementary general music: A survey of teachers' perceptions and practices* (Publication No. 3439183) [Doctoral dissertation, The University of Iowa]. ProQuest Dissertations Publishing.

Ferand, Ernst T. (1940). Improvisation in music history and education. *Papers of the American Musicological Society*, 115–125.

Gatt, Isabelle. (2009). Changing perceptions, practice and pedagogy: Challenges for and ways into teacher change. *Journal of Transformative Education, 7*(2), 164–184. https://doi.org/10.1177/1541344609339024

Gouzouasis, P., & Ryu, J. Y. (2015). A pedagogical tale from the piano studio: Autoethnography in early childhood music education research. *Music Education Research, 17*(4), 397–420. https://doi.org/10.1080/14613808.2014.972924

Grunow, Richard F., Gordon, Edwin E., & Azzara, Christopher D. (1999). *Jump right in: The instrumental series*. GIA Publications.

Hannon, Erin E., & Trehub, Sandra E. (2005). Tuning in to musical rhythms: Infants learn more readily than adults. Proceedings of the National Academy of Sciences of the United States of America, 102(35), 12639–12643. https://doi.org/10.1073/pnas.0504254102

Hopkins, Michael T. (2015). Collaborative composing in high school string chamber music ensembles. *Journal of Research in Music Education, 62*(4), 405–424. https://doi.org/10.1177/0022429414555135

Hopkins, Michael T. (2019). Verification and modification of Fautley's model for analysis of lower secondary school students' group composing processes. *Music Education Research, 21*(1), 71–85. https://doi.org/10.1080/14613808.2018.1503243

Institute for Composer Diversity. (2020). *Orchestra season analysis* [data set]. https://www.composerdiversity.com/orchestra-seasons

Jorgensen, Estelle R. (2008). *The art of teaching music*. Indiana University Press.

Kent, Laura B. (2019). Attaining philosophical alignment: Localizing systemic change through adaptive professional development. *Administrative Issues Journal: Connecting Education, Practice, and Research 9*(2), 1–11. https://doi.org/10.5929/9.2.3

Koops, Alexander P. (2009). *Incorporating music composition in middle school band rehearsals* (Publication No. 3389504) [Doctoral dissertation, University of Southern California]. ProQuest Dissertations Publishing.

Lamaison, Pierre, & Bourdieu, Pierre. (1986). From rules to strategies: An interview with Pierre Bourdieu. *Cultural Anthropology, 1*(1), 110-120. https://www.jstor.org/stable/656327

Mampe, Birgit, Friederici, Angela D., Christophe, Anne, & Wermke, Kathleen (2009). Newborns' cry melody is shaped by their native language. *Current Biology, 19*(23), 1994-1997. https://doi.org/10.1016/j.cub.2009.09.064

Mantie, Roger, & Talbot, Brent C. (2015). How can we change our habits if we don't talk about them? *Action, Criticism, and Theory for Music Education, 14*(1), 128-153. http://act.maydaygroup.org/articles/MantieTalbot14_1.pdf

Mark, Michael L., Gary, Charles L., & Music Educators National Conference. (1999). *A history of American music education* (2nd ed.). MENC.

McNiff, Jean, & Whitehead, Jack. (2005). *Action research for teachers: A practical guide*. David Fulton Publishers. https://doi.org/10.4324/9780203462393

Menard, Elizabeth A. (2015). Music composition in the high school curriculum: A multiple case study. *Journal of Research in Music Education, 63*(1), 114-136. https://doi.org/10.1177/0022429415574310

Mok, Annie O. (2016). A reflective journey in teaching: Pre-service music teachers' action research. *Australian Journal of Music Education, 50*(2), 58-70. https://search.proquest.com/docview/2009457116

Moon, Kyung-Suk. (2006). The commencement of the Manhattanville music curriculum program: 1957-1966. *Journal of Historical Research in Music Education, 27*(2), 71-84. https://doi.org/10.1177/153660060602700202

Nachmanovitch, Stephen. (1990). *Free play: Improvisation in life and art*. J.P. Tarcher, Inc.

Nakata, Takayuki, & Trehub, Sandra E. (2004). Infants' responsiveness to maternal speech and singing. *Infant Behavior and Development, 27*(4), 455-464. https://doi.org/10.1016/j.infbeh.2004.03.002

National Coalition for Core Arts Standards. (2015, April 20). Music tech strand at a glance. https://www.nationalartsstandards.org/sites/default/files/Music%20Tech%20Strand%20at%20a%20Glance%204-20-15.pdf

National Coalition for Core Arts Standards. (2016, July 21). *National core arts standards: A conceptual framework for arts learning*. http://www.nationalartsstandards.org/sites/default/files/Conceptual%20Framework%2007-21-16.pdf

Nicol, David J., & Macfarlane-Dick Debra. (2006). Formative assessment and self-regulated learning: A model and seven principles of good feedback practice. *Studies in Higher Education: 31*(2): 199-218. https://doi.org/10.1080/03075070600572090

Norton, Lin. (2019). *Action research in teaching and learning: A practical guide to conducting pedagogical research in universities* (2nd ed). Routledge.

Piazza, Erik S., & Talbot, Brent C. (in press). Creative musical activities in undergraduate music education curricula. *Journal of Music Teacher Education*.

Robinson, Ken, & Aronica, Lou. (2015). *Creative schools: The grassroots revolution that's transforming education*. Penguin Books.

Robinson, Mitchell. (2015, July 8). *Reformer myth #27: It's not all about the kids....* https://www.mitchellrobinson.net/2015/07/08/reformer-myth-27-it-s-not-all-about-the-kids

Ryan, Richard M., & Deci, Edward L. (2017). *Self-determination theory: Basic psychological needs in motivation, development, and wellness*. The Guilford Press.

Schopp, Steven E. (2006). *A study of the effects of national standards for music education, number 3, improvisation and number 4, composition on high school band instruction in New York State* (Publication No. 3225193) [Doctoral dissertation, Teachers College]. ProQuest Dissertations Publishing.

Schuster, Jack H., & Finkelstein, Martin J. (2008). *The American faculty: The restructuring of academic work and careers*. Johns Hopkins University Press.

Siebert, Johanna J. (2008). *Why music teachers remain in the profession: Conversations with career music educators* (Publication No. 3295324) [Doctoral dissertation, The University of Rochester]. ProQuest Dissertations Publishing.

Slack, Jennifer Daryl, & Wise, J. Macgreggor. (2015). *Culture and technology: A primer* (2nd ed.). Peter Lang Publishing, Inc.

Snell, Alden H., II. (2013). *Creativity in instrumental music education: A survey of winds and percussion music teachers in New York State* (Publication No. 3555065) [Doctoral dissertation, The University of Rochester]. ProQuest Dissertations Publishing.

Stoltzfus, Jay L. (2005). *The effects of audiation-based composition on the music achievement of elementary wind and percussion students.* (Publication No. 3169610) [Doctoral Dissertation, University of Rochester]. ProQuest Dissertations Publishing.

Strand, Katherine. (2006). Survey of Indiana music teachers on using composition in the classroom. *Journal of Research in Music Education, 54*(2), 154–167. https://doi.org/10.1177/002242940605400206

Teach Tomorrow. (2020). *A complete guide to continuing education for teachers.* https://www.teachtomorrow.org/continuing-education-for-teachers

Thomas, Ronald B. (1970). *Manhattanville music curriculum program. Final report.* http://files.eric.ed.gov/fulltext/ED045865.pdf

Trainor, Laurel J., Tsang, Christine D., & Cheung, Vivian H. W. (2002). Preference for sensory consonance in 2- and 4-month-old infants. *Music Perception: An Interdisciplinary Journal, 20*(2), 187–194. https://doi.org/10.1525/mp.2002.20.2.187

Webster, Peter R. (1990). Creativity as creative thinking. *Music Educators Journal, 76*(9), 22–28. https://doi.org/10.2307/3401073

Webster, Peter R. (2016). Creative thinking in music, twenty-five years on. *Music Educators Journal, 102*(3), 26–32. https://doi.org/10.1177/0027432115623841

Whitman, Georann Gale. (2001). *The effects of vocal improvisation on attitudes, aural identification skills, knowledge of music theory, and pitch accuracy in sight-reading of high school choral singers.* (Publication No. 1405142) [Masters thesis, University of Missouri-Kansas City]. ProQuest Dissertations Publishing.

Zitek, J. Samuel. (2008). *An examination of Nebraska high school band directors' implementation of and attitudes toward the national standards in music.* (Publication No. 3331177) [Doctoral dissertation, University of Nebraska]. ProQuest Dissertations Publishing.

About the Authors

Erik Piazza is a Senior Editor at Low Down Publishing and has spent his entire professional life teaching music in upstate New York. He has taught middle school, high school, and collegiate students over the course of his career, and brings many years of practical experience to this book. Erik currently teaches in Webster, NY and is a PhD candidate in music education at the Eastman School of Music.
www.erikspiazza.com

John Mills has taught music in many settings, including public schools, academic conferences, and community groups. Since entering the profession, John has mentored pre-service and early-career music teachers through professional development workshops and practicum experiences. He currently teaches high school classes in music technology, piano, and jazz.
www.mrjohnmills.com

Danny Ziemann is the CEO of Low Down Publishing, and equally passionate as an educator and performer. He taught at the university level for six years, and currently produces jazz bass method books and online video courses. As a jazz musician, he has toured through nearly 20 countries.
www.dannyziemann.com

www.ingramcontent.com/pod-product-compliance
Lightning Source LLC
Chambersburg PA
CBHW031635160426
43196CB00006B/428